gathering

based on a life in progress

This is a work of literature. The truth has been represented as I remember it, with changes made to protect those present in my memories. Events, locales, and conversations have been recreated from my recollections. In some instances, names, identifying characteristics and details such as physical properties, occupations and places of residence, have been changed in order to maintain the anonymity of individuals.

ISBN: 978-0-692-10414-9

For Michael, *solamente una vida*

gathering

Priscilla Thomas

Every time I say, "I'm a writer," I flinch. Over time, it's become internal, almost invisible. But it's there. It's a silent question mark, a wince of the spleen, a bracing for lightning.

Uncomfortable, like shoes that pinch.

When I was ten years old, I went everywhere with a notebook. It was crowded with escape plans and scientific observations on suburban wildlife. Tales of talking clouds interrupted pages of *Harriet the Spy*-esque notes about the neighbors and strangers passing through my days. I grew older, my writing changed: I replaced pages on the peculiar habits of squirrels with studies of how "normal" teenagers behaved, abandoned plotting my ways out in favor of dreamy short fiction featuring young women in far-flung locales, always blissfully, aggressively alone.

Writing had always been the thing that got me through the day. The books I devoured allowed me to slip into new skins. The hip hop and punk rock I wrapped around my head like protective gear gave shape to the living, screaming anger pounding on my ribcage. The stories I wrote were the only way I could see a future for myself. In those pages, I got to live, to say what I could not say out loud about the people who hurt me, my depression, my certainty that I would not survive.

I dreamt of my house by the ocean, my desk by the wide windows, sand permanently nestled into the cracks between the floorboards, and the spaces between my toes, and the fur of the great, shaggy mutt resting at my feet. I dreamed of the stacks of notebooks like treacherous alleys I would expertly navigate to find my way to the kitchen, the bedroom, the sea-facing door. But if you had asked me what I wanted to be, I would never have said, "a writer."

Every July, I spend six hours a day encouraging teachers like me to pick up that title and wear it proudly. Like me, they are mostly uncomfortable, more willing to label themselves as *used-to-be* writers or writing teachers. Sometimes even *aspiring* writers. But writers, straightforward and present-tense, that's tough.

For six hours a day, we do the things that writers do. We write, and we read, and we share our writing with other writers. We compile and revise and reflect. We publish, in voice and in print and digitally. We doubt ourselves and we question our credibility and we hate every word on the page. And then we keep writing.

For six hours a day, for six Julys, I have helped guide six groups of writers toward believing they are writers.

And still, like a writer, I flinch.

Every morning, the "Daily Digest" newsletter from Medium.com sits in my inbox like a letter from my wasted potential. I should just unsubscribe, but I know I won't. Instead I skim the titles of articles I could have written, articles I have almost written, but ultimately articles I have not written, and I sink heavy into my seat. Some people make their livings telling you to be inspired by these moments, turn your failure into fortune, but I am not much motivated by disappointment.

Neither has the changing face of publishing made me hopeful. Despite the ability to submit work to collectives and online magazines, I cling to the letters I received the few times I sent stories off to editors. I accepted those rejections with what I thought was grace, told myself that their opinions were the ones that counted. And now each time I see a link to a post on Thought Catalog that seems to have been lifted from my subway musing the week before, I don't even feel indignant. Only deflated, moaning from my slump on the couch, "I should be writing! Right now!"

One such day, after such moaning, Kris called out, "What are you talking about?"

I held out my phone, as if he could see it from two rooms away, and resumed whining. "All these stories, these pieces. I could be writing them. I should be. I don't know why I'm not. I don't know why every time I sit down to write, nothing happens."

I had more, about how this was my *job* and this was what I tried to teach teenagers *and* adults but I couldn't seem to do for *myself*, but he walked over to me, ignoring the offering of my phone, the displayed proof of my mediocrity.

"What do you count?" he asked me.

I frowned, not sure what he meant. He continued: he had been reading what I had been writing every day for the past two weeks. Writing and publishing, he told me. And it wasn't just him reading, he said. People, he told me, read what you write. They like it, they tell you they like it, they share it and thank you for it.

He was referring to a thing I was doing on Instagram, #30daysofstories. The hashtag had appeared on my feed care of Jen Sinkler, a woman I follow and admire who is best known for her presence in the world of fitness and strength training. She's also a writer, and the first time I met her, we delved into the stickiness of complexity: how we struggle to balance the varied identities that we claim, how we rationalize being all of the things that we are; how we decide which foot to put forward and which will stay behind. Jen had put her writer foot forward, sharing a vibrant slice-of-life that I reread 20 times, each time thinking, *I want to do this.*

I enjoyed the format of photo and story. The character limits required me to craft and re-craft, to allow poetry to seep into the spaces left by truncated sentences. Sometimes, the stories felt like letters I was writing to a younger me, like a warm hand on my back.

"But –" I started to say. He looked at me knowingly. I had been about to say it, that they didn't count. His eyebrows were cocked, mirrored in a slight smirk that asked me, *Well, what does?*

When the *Hamilton* mixtape dropped, it was "Wrote My Way Out" that served as my anthem – Nas, Dave East, and Lin-Manuel Miranda recounting stories of the triumph and mobility writing provided, while Aloe Blacc crooned a warm honey hook about how words save us when people cannot.

It was like the song had been written for me, speaking the ghost of my adolescent self back into existence: the ever-present notebook, the curtain of hair behind which I hid, watched, dreamed, composed.

As much as I loved the song, I felt fraudulent. I couldn't stop thinking about all I hadn't done: the files I've deleted and notebooks I've destroyed, the unpublished stories and articles, the editors' business cards I've left to fade in junk drawers, the abandoned blogs.

Alone in a room, the song playing for the fifth time in a row while I graded or cleaned or toweled dry, I'd throw back my head and crow along: "I picked up a pen...and I wrote my way OWWWT!"

And deep inside, still smiling, I would flinch.

One morning in the Bronx, an elderly woman asked me for directions to Story Av. She spoke to me in Spanish, the words water fast and comfortably softened. There was no doubt in her mind that I could understand her and reply. Instead of shying away as I usually did at that point of my language acquisition, I stumbled through an explanation, flailing my hands around the concepts I could not express (like transferring to the 2 train by crossing the street and walking one block). The woman thanked me in English, grasping my hands in hers and telling me in Spanish, "I believed you were mine."

Dazzled and full-hearted, I opened Facebook to relay the anecdote and accompanying observations on how this language and culture have shaped my identity, embraced me in my voluntary estrangement from my family, broadened my horizons.

"I didn't know you were a writer!" people kept telling me, in comments and messages, to my red, twitching face.

"I'm so glad you're still writing," other people told me, people who had known me from notebook days, from college classes, from LiveJournal communities.

I shrugged, helpless, uncertain, words pooling in my upturned hands.

Stubbornly, weeds through concrete, my writing has survived. It has clung to me, winding sturdy vines around me. With tending, it bursts into bloom, flourishing under the attention. I realize that I cannot pluck it out any more than I could unseat my beating heart. All I can do is nourish it. Collect it. Gather it, unflinching, in my arms.

rosebuds

growing

It started with tomatoes, seeds tiny and delicate as the wings of gnats nearly invisible in our palms. We pressed them into paper cups of soil and gazed down at the spots where they disappeared, and I thought that this was the definition of faith: putting hope into the soft earth and trusting the darkness. I smiled to myself but I didn't say it out loud. I was still shy about my daydreaminess in front of Kris, and everyone.

I told stories to the unfolding sprouts, marveling at how their creases softened every day. I woke up on weekend mornings at Kris's apartment and sat beside their damp, rich, growing smell, stroking their tender leaves. Their scent, their vibrant green, reminded me of my parents' garden. As a kid, I would hide in the foliage for hours, pretending I was a wild thing, eating strawberries the size of my fingertips until their sweetness stung my tongue.

The tomatoes grew taller, some bushy and sprawling while others were gangly in their adolescence. Kris teased me about favoring those reedy plants, cupping their wobbly heads and murmuring encouragement to them (they took all my chill, honestly). When we transferred them from their yogurt cup homes to our new window box, I cradled their roots tenderly, supporting their delicate bodies as we packed the soil down around their fragile ends. I held my breath each time I let my hands float away and watched them stand up on their own. By summer, we would lean out under their tangled vines, ease our hands through their curls to detach their sunwarm fruits.

When they withered in the fall, I mourned their brittle brown vines until we found Monster Basil, a castoff plant that grew to overtake the kitchen window and resurrected itself for years. Then came the habanero plants that we admired and feared, tending to them in the same way you navigate a room with a wasp in it. The window box grew wild on our fire escape, sometimes bursting with unchecked growth, sometimes housing only skeletons.

"What do you think will happen if I put these strawberry tops in the dirt?" Kris asks, and I shrug and smile, handing him an empty flowerpot.

My parents had gardened with purpose, with an understanding of seasons and aesthetics. They planned – no whims or surprises, all zoning and menus. I, on the other hand, stop outside a corner store on my way to the train because some small potted thing has gleaming fruit or pretty leaves. The proprietor and I mime our way through a language barrier – "Eat?" I ask, bringing my hand from leaf to mouth. "No eat!" he warns, striking the air in front of me as if beating back a flame. I arrive home, beaming amid the

fronds bursting from my arms, and we welcome the newest
additions to our homemade jungle.

new york, new york

I don't love New York. 12 years into this relationship, I wake up in the city I dreamed of and feel tired. Empty. I think about it, what brought me here, the charm that wound its fingers around my heart and pulled me closer, beat by beat. Then I look around at the storefronts and buildings that have been replaced or covered up by new, shiny, $15 for small plates restaurants, the pushy, sneering 20-somethings who have lived here for a few months and think walking in The City means playing human bumper cars. I watch herds of upward-gazing tourists amble across my path and long for the comparatively empty sidewalks of this avenue pre-"discovery." *Go home*, I think one thousand times a day, never quite sure who I'm talking to.

I grew up in New Jersey, but for an embarrassingly long time, I cherished the fact that I'd been born in New York City. My family moved to New Jersey when I was close to a year old; I have no memories of the Washington Heights apartment where the five of us and my aunt were crowded together. This never stopped me from telling my classmates and new acquaintances that I was *from* New York, but I now lived in New Jersey. Every first day of school ice breaker was an opportunity for me to establish my origin story and to lay out the path ahead of me. New Jersey was my present, but I knew where I had come from and where I would return.

"This doesn't even feel like we're in New York," I complained in my best cool-and-bored tone. I gestured to the flashing billboards above us, leaned back against the wall, and shrugged. My roommate, Gigi, rolled her eyes before agreeing with me. Times Square wasn't my idea, but here we were. We were 15, spending six weeks of our summer at Columbia University, discovering for the first time the freedom of a MetroCard in hand. Gigi was from central NJ and she had been to the city before: gone to Broadway, South St. Seaport. She had been a tourist, as the NYC natives in our program would put it.

My New York connection was more credible, even to the natives. My parents' jobs and past lives uptown gave me a different, more frequent exposure; we lived close by, grocery shopped and bought back-to-school clothes on Dyckman when we wanted a deal, and my dad still sometimes got Dominican takeaway for dinner. Our small town somehow had a direct bus to the city, and I would sneak off to shows or to wander, exploring the lower grid between Irving and Mars Bar (where the bouncer just laughed as he shooed me away), perfecting a mask of indifference as I clutched my just-in-case cell phone in my pocket.

Gigi, plus our suitemates and the boys across the hall, went along with my aimless approach to seeing the city because I had that imagined cred. We walked river to river, got lost in the Villages and Central Park, took turns choosing random stops to spill off the train past disgruntled commuters. We always did keep our promise to our RA to stay out of Morningside and Riverside Parks, though.

When I moved to New York after college, I rented the top floor of a house in the Bronx, near the end of the 4 train. Many of my fellow new teachers had apartments in the area, these cavernous spaces that our college dorm furniture was too small and awkward to fit into – not unlike us, barely adults and trying to pretend we belonged at the heads of our classrooms. The end of that first school year meant changes for many of us, and it started me on my tradition of moving almost every year.

I left the Bronx for East Harlem, back when real estate agents were struggling to make "SpaHa" a thing. A new developer buying up the area and employing slumlord tactics to drive out the long-term residents sent me and my college best friend to the Upper East Side. We were miserable, and she was living in a closet, so we kept moving. I finally settled for a while in a place of my own back in Spanish Harlem, where "SpaHa" was thankfully still not a thing.

All this time, I really loved New York. It was crowded and loud and it wanted all of my money, but I loved it. Garbage overflowed its containers; streets and subway cars stank of urine; men followed me when I ignored their shouted propositions and bystanders gave me the dirty looks for it;

when I sat in the park by my apartment on the Upper East Side, women interrupted my reading to ask after the whereabouts of the child they assumed I was caring for. It didn't matter. I loved this city. It was the only place for me.

Still, I never thought I'd live in Midtown – it was so far from what I knew as New York. My work had always been the Bronx, heart and home always uptown. *RENT* and punk had instilled a deep love for Alphabet City, but I'd always skipped the middle. It was for outsiders and newcomers, not for me. Nothing about it appealed to me, until I met Kris.

I take the train a stop north of what Google would tell me so I can walk home without navigating the crush of bodies that fills Times Square. Working in Queens now, my trains move sideways and the game of tracing my way along colorful threads on the map takes me back to playing navigator in the passenger seat of my family's pale blue Thunderbird. I learn new ways to avoid the bustle, routes and connections that convenience algorithms won't put together.

And still, some late nights I find myself on the opposite subway platform and realizing it is like waking up with a sudden start. Sometimes the Frankenstein address I have absentmindedly written on a form or letter consists of pieces from all of my New York City homes. Sometimes, I miss a stop and get off at 42nd, and when I find myself on the fringe of these neon glows, I wonder how on earth I got here.

Knuckles sits in his lawn chair outside of the dry cleaner's storefront, face folded as he squints at the passing pedestrians. Another neighborhood old timer sidles over, unfolds his own chair beside him. They talk in faded, papery voices as they watch the street and I wonder if they, like me, are asking themselves why they're still here. I dismiss that question as soon as it surfaces; I know I'm just another new transplant stomping through their neighborhood, never nodding or saying hello. I don't know if I belong or if I'll stay.

For now, I look forward to what is mine: the smiling faces in the bread shop, the homemade soup waiting in the kitchen (*our* kitchen), the chirruping cats who have never had so much room to gallop and will rush to greet me when I climb the stairs (our stairs) and open all the doors (our doors) so I can watch them run. Sometimes I arrive to find no one and sometimes all three of mine are waiting as I turn the stubborn lock, and each time I step inside I feel like I am home.

I asked my students, "What's something that you love about yourself?" I had practiced my answer the night before, trying out possible responses and shooting them down as untrue, vain, inaccessible. I finally settled on an answer that I thought could work, and then I prepared a few follow-up questions to prompt students who didn't know what to say.

It had been awhile since we had a Circle, a practice of Restorative Justice that encourages the development of listening, sharing, being open, and creating safe environments in classrooms. They can be amazing, and they can be terrifying, and they can be just fine. Of course, the ones I hear the most about and spend the most time thinking about are at the ends of the spectrum: fantastic or disastrous. My advisees and I usually have decent circles, though I sometimes have to forcibly unfocus my perfectionist's lens in order to appreciate them.

My 15 advisees were 9th graders, most in their first year in the US. We spoke six languages between us, with English as a soft overlap. Circles had been challenging, trying to navigate language, emotions, and maturity levels. I was ready for them to complain, to draw blanks, and to make me break out my teacher face a few times during this Circle.

"What's something you love about yourself?" I asked, and after clarifying and translating, all 15 of them began to write. They turned to the nearest classmate to practice reading their statements in English. I stared around the circle at them, wondering who these children were. A small group of them conferred with the rest and announced they were all ready to share. "Who has the talking piece?" someone asked and I handed it – a palm-sized figurine of Wonder Woman – over silently. 14 faces turned expectantly to the first speaker, Davi, who placed Wonder Woman in Fatou's waiting palm with a reverent softness. Even as they snuck looks down at their cards during someone's sharing, the whole group applauded after each person shared.

Julia turned to me after sharing her list, gently placing the plastic doll in my hand. I closed my fingers over hers for a moment, feeling tears begin to pool at the corners of my eyes and not even minding that they might spill over.

I was halfway through my workday when I realized that I would be coming home to an empty apartment for the first time since Kris and I moved in together. I go away for weekend conferences sometimes, but this time I was the one to stay behind.

"What are you going to do differently?" Pooja asked me, after classes ended.

I shrugged, grinned. "Stay at work forever?" I gestured to the papers and laptop spread before me. We laughed.

The night before, I had dreamed of restless feet pacing the empty rooms of the apartment, hurrying always just ahead of me, disappearing before I could catch their owners. In the morning, the cats rushed past me at the open door. I found them on the bed, sniffing, pressing tentative paws on the undisturbed side of the sheets as if he were hiding deep inside, ready to pounce. Chirping, squawking, they turned to me in wonder.

On my way home from work, he texted me, 'Are you home? I wanted to call you.' I rang him on speaker as I washed dishes and he drove around looking for elusive Taco Bells. I wondered if he could hear the smile in my voice, my breath coming shorter as my heart skipped and fluttered.

He told me about his day, parked the car to wander the downtown on foot. Twice, I stopped myself from asking him when he was coming home, forgetting.

"What streets are you at right now?" I asked. He paused, answered. "Ok, there's a Taco Bell, like, seven minutes away from you."

He walked back to the car, jogging when he saw that the blue bags covering the meters were printed with warnings. There was no ticket, a small miracle giving his record on our vacations. I read him directions as he drove. He called me a stalker. The cats called out to me from the far end of the apartment, still searching.

homeland

I kept checking our flight confirmations, largely because I couldn't believe we would be flying directly from New York to Mumbai. Growing up, my family's once-every-five-years trips to Kerala always included European layovers – Brussels, Berlin, London. I relished those hours in the airports: the welcome legroom, wandering through the clusters of chatter in French, Spanish, German, sprawling out at cafe tables to read books (and when I was 18, ordering a completely legal yet totally exhilarating wine from a waiter who delivered my 'glass of red' with a smirk and a square of chocolate).

The stopover was a friendly transition, a sigh between the hustle of JFK boarding and the upcoming crush of people, movement, and heat that was the Mumbai Airport. Preparation. We wouldn't have that this time, and as I anticipated the chaos, I realized that I was approaching this trip the way I had always approached a visit "home" – hands braced against the dash in front of me, holding in my breath with every muscle in my body as I readied myself for impact.

I hadn't been to India in nearly 15 years. I expected never to go again, certainly not to Cochin. I had always figured if Kris and I made it to India, we would visit Delhi, take the train up the Himalayas. Kerala was a greyed-out area of the map in my mind.

In cutting myself off from my family of origin, I felt I had drawn a line between myself and my cultural home; it never felt like a place that wanted me, anyway. Clinging to my parents as the cascading Malayalaam conversations surrounded and overwhelmed me, I was rude for not being able to respond to people's questions. As a punk-loving teenager, I rendered my cousins' eager attempts to discuss American pop music as fruitless as their questions about my thoughts on recent Bollywood films. Among my extended family, I was always too withdrawn, too chubby, too American, too soft.

Kerala was beautiful, sky and plants and canals in vibrant colors that seemed to ripen in the dense heat. It was home, where our visits would bring crowds of relatives to my grandparents' homes to sleep on the floor, where every aunty wanted to cup my growing face in her hands and set before me plates of food that redefined flavor and fulfillment. And it was lonely, one more place I did not quite belong, one more place I could not figure out.

So, as our departure date drew nearer and nothing was booked, and my search history stacked up with queries like *best dosa in cochin, what to wear in kerala,* and, *thekkady no tour,* I found myself whispering, "Breathe." I have never known who I am in Kerala, who I need to be, who I am allowed to be. And as scared as I was, I was also somewhat excited to start finding out.

"Your hair's different," Kris said, one week prior to our trip. He had woken up to find me seated at our dining table, black curls still damp from the shower. The sweet ammonia scent of boxed hair dye lingered. Coloring over my pink hair had been an attempt to feel more prepared and less anxious about returning to Kerala, which is politely referred to as "conservative" by white travel bloggers. They gently suggest that other white travelers wear slightly longer shorts when visiting. For me, nothing above the knee was getting near the suitcase.

Growing up, I was already self-conscious about my changing body and its insistent curvaceousness. At home, at school, among relatives, my body itself was labelled as provocative and indecent. A visit to Kerala guaranteed weeks of having my appearance even more intensely criticized and policed. The idea of sweating under long pants and tunics with summer shorts off-limits brought up some initial resistance in me: I wanted to be a wanton American tourist, for once. But also, I wanted to see Kerala as I had never been able to see it – sans obligations to my family and their name, up close and at my own pace.

My Western-ness cannot be disguised; it is announced by my asymmetrical hair, my tattoos, my deliberately darkened skin, my boyfriend. And it can create walls. My exposed legs and pink hair, I decided uneasily, would do nothing to bridge the gulf that will always exist between my identity and my ancestry.

Due to "technical issues" on our jumbo jet, we and our 350+ fellow travelers spent about seven hours waiting on the plane and in the terminal to hear that our flight to Mumbai was officially cancelled. Then came a few more hours of lines, handwritten lists of names that would somehow get us rooms at an airport hotel, commandeered shuttle buses that drove us to the airport hotel of another airport, and no wake-up calls or notifications of our rescheduled flights leaving us scrambling for a cab to get us back to the airport on time.

"It's a decent warm-up for traveling in India," I joked to Kris and some fellow travelers. The trip ahead would put us in uncomfortable situations for which there would be little prior experience to inform our decisions; it would demand we shift our perspectives and check our timelines at the door; it would push us to reach out to strangers across barriers of language and insecurity; it would require us to acknowledge our smallness in the world. These are hallmarks of a great, life-affirming trip, and we hadn't even left the country yet.

That night, we wedged ourselves into a rickety former Access-a-Ride van with ten other displaced passengers and a driver who had never been to the hotel we were meant to find. We were close, but a bit lost, when one of the passengers began navigating, reading out directions from his phone. A few other men took up a chorus, shouting over the rattle of the van, the rush of air through the windows, the radio that alternated between crackling static and blaring Reggaeton. When the driver missed a turn, the navigator said, "OK, my friend, continue straight and we will take the next left" ("NEXT LEFT!" cried the chorus). At the hotel, what little news was available, and reassurances, traveled up and down the line for check-in. It had been like this back at the airport, passengers directing one another, waving people over to the proper boarding lines, sharing information as they received snippets from airline personnel. "Somehow," I had said at the hotel, "we'll all get there."

As we waited to board our rescheduled flight, Kris said that a lot of things made more sense to him now. The way people helped one another, made folk by the shared experience. We had traveled big circles since the day before, but even as I settled again into the middle seat of the red and gold AirIndia jet, it didn't feel like we had arrived in the same place.

runaway

I found the bag one summer morning, in the downstairs closet, a neglected scrap of space under the stairs that was crammed with winter coats and ugly sweaters in plastic storage. Everything in the closet smelled strongly of mothballs, except for this soft leather tote. Its scent reminded me of earth and baking bread, and it felt like the smooth skin on the back of my mother's upper arms.

I had just completed 3rd grade, but I had been planning how to run away for years by then. As a smaller child, my escape attempts were spontaneous and daring, darting away in the grocery store or squirming free as my mother tried to force my stiff, stubborn limbs into party clothes. I would bolt into the yard in no more than underpants, making for the street as quickly as my chubby legs could toddle me. One of my brothers, a year older, was always just behind me, having quickly taken on the role of my wrangler. He could usually tackle me by the edge of the yard and sit on me until one of my parents came to carry me inside, though once I made it halfway down the block before my father caught up. My brother must have been on the potty.

As I got older, I planned more seriously, as was becoming of a bright, well-read young woman. I kept a list in the back of my writing notebook. The list was divided into three columns

– Location, Pro, and Con – and covered several pages. It was written on and over many times; some entries were thoroughly crossed out, some circled, and a few had arrows leading to additional notes crammed into margins and between items. My research was mostly observational, with a lot of supplementation from things I heard adults saying and stories I read.

I kept a list of Ideal Conditions, too (dark/boring clothing, daytime, crowded place, distractions, multiple exits, shortly after a meal). It was a phrase I had picked up from a TV movie about soldiers, or maybe spies, and I had started making the list the same day that I saw the movie. Someday, I knew, the opportunity would present itself, and I intended to be ready.

The bag was big, but it was perfect. I tenderly stroked the soft leather of the tote, peeked inside to admire the many zippered pockets hidden in the lining. Walking with it was difficult – it would collide with my elbow and snag in the fold of my knee – but I knew I just needed to practice. I darted up to my room with the bag to consult another list in my notebook: Go Bag Supplies.

Being eight years old, I didn't have access to the funds I would need to stock my go bag, so I had to be creative, and secretive. I moved slowly, hoping my parents would not notice the disappearance of small items.

Maybe my father figured his second best flashlight had been misplaced in the shuffle of tools from his workshop to the car and back, and my mother simply assumed she had used the canned goods that were gone from the pantry, adding them to the grocery list again. The hand rake from the garden was asked after a few times, but the same concern did not touch the nylon rope I had discovered in the shed behind our house. I tied the knots carefully, yanking on the slack to ensure my homemade grappling hook wouldn't slip mid-climb.

The pepper spray was also DIY: hot sauce poured into a bottle of body spray I'd received as a birthday gift. I emptied out the perfume, but its bubble gum scent remained and mixed oddly with the vinegary odor of Tabasco. I worried the smell would soak into the bag, so I filled the interior pockets with newspaper and dryer sheets.

I carried the bag everywhere with me that summer, the supplies pressed into the bottom of the tote and hidden beneath a scarf my mother had given me for playing dress-up. It was mostly used as a tourniquet for imagined wounds, but it made an excellent cover for the go bag.

On top of it, I laid decoy items: lip gloss and hair clips and cute fluffy toys on keychains, a book, a pack of colored markers. I practiced hiding how much heavier the bag was than how it

Location	Pro	Con
airport	- very busy, crowded - places to get lost - distracting goodbyes - easy to blend in	- makes Mom nervous - expensive tickets - can't follow people onto planes - security
bus station	- easy to hide in bathroom - no one paying attention - cheap tickets	→ smelly - maybe won't sell me a ticket - police next door - not a lot of kids
mall	- crowded - lots of distractions - easy to blend in	- nowhere to go after - security and cameras - kids alone get helped or yelled at
cities	- very crowded - easy to blend - distractions - easy to follow groups - trains and buses - not weird alone - busy - cheap food ($1 hot dogs)	- dangerous, need protection - pickpockets - dirty

A reproduction

seemed, lifting it smoothly to my shoulder while I kept my face relaxed in the mirror. Most nights before I fell asleep, I went over items on my lists in my head, preparing.

mistakes

Malia winced every time my pen touched the paper. Hakeem couldn't watch, flipping restlessly through a dictionary he had grabbed from the shelf he passed on his way to my desk.

"How's that book?" I asked, smirking.

He nodded, turning another page as his gaze wandered the far wall. "Good, good."

They had asked me for this — fix the errors, show me what to do — but it was brutal. I felt like I should have known better than to give in.

"Mistakes are good," I said, my oft-repeated line. "We need mistakes. You can't grow unless you make them."

I assured them that I make mistakes when I write, all the time. I told them about a blog post I had written, the drafting I had done with my friends, how my writing had been taken apart and reassembled and cut back into pieces.

Malia smiled, nodded thoughtfully, but Hakeem shrugged. He spoke to the dictionary in front of him. "Your mistakes and our mistakes are different."

I was struck, silent for a moment, reminded of every time a teacher or classmate said that something I was struggling with was "easy." Hakeem looked up from the dictionary and held my eyes, reflecting the irritation and helplessness that followed those assurances. I had forgotten this. How trying to make someone feel better is often dismissive. How it doesn't work.

"You're right," I said, when my breath returned. I put my fist over my heart, the way he would when he tried to challenge twice-his-height-and-width Ahmed to a competition of strength. "That is what makes you brave."

And at least he smiled.

a kerala woman

On only our second day in Cochin, I lay in bed feeling like I couldn't move. The pressure of the disapproval I had started to collect in public spread across me like a heavy blanket. I had fully expected side-eye in preparing for this trip. I knew we would attract attention and I knew not all of it would be positive or curious. But the openly hostile stares of young men and older women, the sneers and unbroken gazes, were surprisingly hard to bear. On our first walk outside the hotel, it startled both of us. "People look at you more than they look at me," Kris observed. I nodded mutely.

I knew I would look ridiculous to some – an obviously Kerala girl, plump, in American outfits, with a lopsided haircut – but I was infuriating to others. Men turned over their shoulders while walking so as not to disrupt their glowering; women made the faces of tasting sour milk. I was somewhat surprised to see these other, familiar faces in Cochin, what we had always called "the city." But it wasn't unfamiliar: this feeling, those faces.

On the third day, I stood before the mirror in our hotel room, recalling the vicious eyes an aunty had cut at my ankles, exposed by my maxi dress, and shrugged. We set out into the city on foot, taking turns off the main drag until we had forgotten how many and in which order.

Beside us, behind us, mopeds, tuk-tuks, cars, and buses raced by for any scrap of open road, and we shifted to the side without stopping. The smell of hot bread called us will to a local restaurant where the proprietor stood, shocked by our presence (wife urging him from behind: "What would you like, say. Say!"). In a few moments, we bent over warm roti and saucers of beef curry like my grandmother used to make, steaming glasses of chai to mellow out the slow burn of the chilies. We sat, watching an old man stretch chapathi dough with deft flicks of his wrist, listening to the light chatter of neighbors coming in for tea and sweet plantain fritters, and for a moment I felt I had found a way back home.

Our next stop was Kumily town, of Thekkady, where tourists are not unusual. North Indian women wear sleeveless tops and skinny jeans; Europeans glow like snow sprinkled across the landscape. We sat in the "French restaurant," a one-room cement structure at the edge of a chicken-pecked lot where you could sometimes order baguettes, with rotating groups of backpacking twenty-somethings who raised my hackles without even trying (but, oh, it felt like they were trying).

I wore jeans, my second time ever wearing them in India; they felt so strange and I had to force myself not to touch my own butt too often, to check that it was covered. I took the safety pins out of my scarves and let them drape instead of diligently securing their coverage. Little by little, I relaxed.

Men still turned to stare at me in disbelief and one group of young people out for an evening sat directly behind us and talked in exaggerated whispers about us – snippets of Malayalam and English darted at my ears like so many hungry fish. But people were kinder. There was of course the appeal of the money we would spend, but there was also a general warmth that Cochin did not hold for me. When a group of men on their way to a "safari" ride hung out of their jeep to stare wonderingly into our passing tuk-tuk, I found that I could laugh. There is a certain pride in being more fascinating than a Sambar deer.

I am accustomed to justifying, explaining, and defending my Indian-ness. Everything from my name to my tastes to my apparently wrong bilingualism becomes evidence against my cultural heritage.

These days, I'm more direct: My parents are from India; I was born here. It never feels like enough. I have never felt Indian enough, whatever that means. From family to friends to strangers, I've never lacked for people to point out all of the ways I didn't fit in, all of the reasons I could not claim my Indian identity.

Returning to Kerala without any family ties was healing. The beginning stages of healing, when it hurts worse than the wound, but healing still. Malayalam seeped back into my brain, and I found myself following overheard conversations better than I expected, the words for things swimming into my mind just as I need them. The sneers and scowls that met me at every turn in Cochin were replaced by curiosity and sometimes even delight in Thekkady. I got good at saying, "Amma from Kottayam, Appa from Perumbavoor," when people turned to me for a second, Where are you from? They smiled, told me anecdotes about visits or relatives from the same areas. They asked how long it had been since I'd visited and they welcomed me back when I told them.

When our guide at the tea factory turned to me and said, "You look like a Kerala woman," I couldn't ignore the leaping sensation of my heart, the satisfaction that surged up inside of me. It was a fragment, a moment, a step closer to myself.

holding

"It's ok to ask for what you need," Serena tells me. It's Friday, we're standing in the hallway between our classrooms marveling at how we got here. The week has been ages. "I know I need approval, and he knows that, too. I had to make that really clear: I need to know what I did well and I need feedback to come soon." I fidget. I recognize myself in the picture she is drawing and I don't like it.

I'm coming to terms with my appetite for validation, the desire to be identified by others as 'ok' or 'good enough.' Whether it's body or beauty, work or art, I can usually find a piece of me holding her breath, waiting for some authority to deem it worthy. It's not a new discovery, but it was something of a revelation when I found it, like the first time you realize that breathing just happens and then you choke and gasp because thinking about breathing has made you stop doing it for a moment. It's like that: vital, default.

"I can't just tell myself to stop doing what I do, or being who I am," Serena says. "So, it's something we work with."

I think about summertime, clamping our jaws down to hold

full lungs just under the surface of the water until the growing heat in our chests was too much. We burst the surface in an explosion of dramatics, gulping air and crying out, but immediately turned to the timekeeper to find out how many hippopotami we needed to win the next round. Ready, already, to try again.

I play a game like this with approval, with not seeking it. I share writing or photos or doodles, knowing that they won't be loved and validated, or not knowing at all. and then I walk away. Sometimes, it crumbles, the thing I created and enjoyed. I tear it down, tuck the pieces away. Sometimes, I go back to look at it, adore it, over and over. It depends, maybe on me. What I think.

Serena pushes me. Not only her; the world around me is filled with echoes and patterns. People push me, to accept, to own what is mine. Like the stories in my body, like the air in my lungs.

sincerely

Dear Miller,

I love telling people how long I have known you, putting the years into terms of schools and boroughs. When you say to Lily that we have been friends since we were "baby teachers," her little piggy squeals of laughter just crack me open. And so it has been hard, trying to wrangle the words to tell you that you are scaring me.

When Lily could only babble, you had conversations with her. You listened to her rambling strings of sounds, her emphatic monologues of noises, and you replied. Asked her questions. She would fix her somber hazel eyes on you, breathe in deeply through her tiny nose, and continue. There was nothing you didn't want to hear, nothing you would ever silence, no box to which you would confine her.

Meanwhile, it seems that the walls you assemble around the students in your classroom become closer, more solid, every few months. There is less air, less space for their voices, and you claim to be listening but when you quote them, their words sound so much like yours.

I find myself preparing to lose you. Already, I spend our infrequent visits dreading the moment you will bring up the conversation of school, of standards, of "The English Classroom." I sit on the floor with Lily and brace myself for the impact of your most recent *observations* and *new understandings*. I am knocked off balance anyway.

It's not an irrational hypersensitivity, not (only) my prejudice against the ideologies of the school where you now work, or blind allegiance to public schools and unions. I am not deluded, thinking that the school where we cut our teeth was a pinnacle of excellence, or even of functionality. I am afraid, of who you are becoming and how you have begun to think.

Dear Alva,

I think often of the night we celebrated your 27th birthday in the Upper East Side, dropping to the back of the crowd as we ambled from one bland, overgrown frat-house bar to the next. Ahead of us, our friends were boisterous, whooping through the spring evening.

You told me that the police officer who shot Charles Kinsey as he lay on the ground, unarmed and compliant with his arms overhead, said, "I don't know." Shot, Kinsey had cried out, "Why?" and the officer replied, "I don't know."

The officer who murdered Philando Castile was reported to have said the same, initially: "I don't know."

As our friends bounced ahead, we huddled close and whispered about the officer who shot Kinsey, the officers who wrongfully arrested Patrick Furman after brutalizing him outside of his home, the officers who had shot over 40 civilians in the few months since Alton Sterling was executed in a parking lot next to his makeshift CD stand.

"Do any of them know?" we asked, of no one, of the night air, of the backs of our coworkers and friends as we walked along. "Did any of them understand what it means to shoot someone – what *could*, what *will* happen? Do they know now?"

Your eyes looked like mine felt: wide and tired and too bright.

Dear Micah, Ebony, Neema, Jason, Ava, Yoli,

I know that many of you did not love me, even hated me, for not being who you thought I should be. You wanted more strictness, more calls home, more templates to fill in, more written work with my judgements in the margins. You wanted more practice exams, less writing through the uncertainty. You wanted the guarantee that I had 10 simple steps to make you Good Writers, the assurance that what we were doing would be on The Test, the hard proof that our classroom was making you College Ready.

I'm sorry I allowed you to believe that your worth was tied to an exam that everyone in your life would stop caring about in two years. I'm sorry I believed what I was told to expect of you instead of giving you the space to set those expectations yourself. I'm sorry that I doubted myself so much that it extended to you, too.

I think you needed fewer reasons why our class mattered, and more proof that you mattered. I'm sorry that I couldn't hold onto myself more tightly, that I couldn't believe in what I knew and help you see it, too.

I know that I already had my chance to be your teacher, but I wish I could share one more lesson with you. It is one I am only beginning to feel like I'm learning, but it may be the most important one I've attempted. I wish I could have more time to work alongside you as we grappled with identity and self-acceptance, with accepting others.

I wish I could tell you this: the angry, sharp pieces you have carried inside of you are not *you*, they are not *forever*, and they do not make you unworthy. I wish I had given you more tools and more time to start putting those pieces together, to reshape and reflect on yourselves.

If we had more time, I would say over and over again: you deserve to like what you see when you look at yourself. You deserve words – their sanctuary and their release.

Dear Fernando,

I remember that Monday you came in early – way early, close to an hour before first period. You leaned around the edge of my doorway and asked me if I had a minute, you just needed to tell me that you were sorry you hadn't done your weekend homework. I laughed and said, "Fernando, you have literally *never* done your weekend homework."

And then you told me that you had been arrested and held in a cell for two days that weekend.

You sat in the back of the room, and you told me that Mrs. G in the office had asked you, "What did you do?" And she said to you, "Police don't just arrest people for no reason."
I remember how we sat there with the lights off so no one would come in until you stopped crying and felt ready to walk to the cafeteria. I wanted to go to the office, to go to Mrs. G and tell her about all of it. I wanted to yell at her. But I didn't. I think I didn't want to find out how she would react, what her face would do.

I'm sorry.

Instead, I went back to my dark classroom and thought about my weekend, how I came across two police officers lining up five neighborhood boys against the metal grate of a store on my block. Two of the boys, brothers it seemed, were squeezing each other's hands. The younger boy's face was shivering with the effort of controlling his brimming eyes. He was breathing frantically through his nose, a staccato rhythm that my heartbeat picked up and echoed. One of the officers ordered them over and over to let go of each other's hands. The boy on the end jumped every time.

I had stood frozen on my corner, until the officers told them all to go straight home. Both officers looked at me as they got into their car like I was something stuck to their shoes, something they wanted to scrape against the curb.

I thought about how I had been holding my breath on that corner, and I realized I was doing it again. I hadn't breathed since I had sat down in the dark classroom. I exhaled in a sigh so low I barely felt it.

I think about this moment a lot, Fernando. I wonder how I would act if I could do it again, how I would behave now. I feel like I'm still holding that breath.

Dear Lea,

When I think about how I contributed to a system that endeavored to stifle you, that demanded your compliance over your curiosity, I feel ill. We failed you. Even when you gave in and tried to do what was asked of you, we continued to fail you. We told you it was too little, too late, when we had been expecting *only* too little of you. We failed you over and over, and then held out our hands, waiting for you to engage in learning from your mistakes. But they weren't yours to learn from. We should have been helping you harness your voice instead of gagging you for four years and demanding you to sing out when the knot was finally undone.

I'm sorry I didn't know how to fight for you, and that I couldn't teach you to fight for yourself.

Dear Miller,

I don't want to lose you. You are funny, and kind, and smart, and unmatched on the dance floor. Maybe you'll think all of this is unfair of me. Maybe in and of themselves, these comments and moments are not so damning. These are out of context, you might think. That's true.

But what else are you thinking? Are you remembering the students with whom you've clashed and written off? Are you thinking of the doors you've closed on them, the kids you've refused to understand? Do you think about who they are now, and what they're doing? Do you wonder about the former teachers of brutalized, buried young people?

I believe that you care about me, Miller, and about your students, about our lives. But I wonder if you worry about losing them.

Sincerely.

likeness

When I was about 10 years old, my friend Jenny came back from a summer trip to the shore with the coolest souvenirs from the boardwalk – all the awesome junk my parents would never waste their money on. My father's only approved boardwalk purchase was a tin of salt water taffy; classics only, no fun flavors allowed. Jenny, on the other hand, came back with beaded bracelets up to the elbow, airbrushed t-shirts with Looney Tunes on them, and even a Water Weenie. (Though, I wasn't jealous really of that one; they grossed me out.)

The true prize of her trip was a boardwalk caricature. Her comically enlarged head on her petite cartoon body was delightful – she looked so delicate and goofy. I had to have one. I knew my parents would never agree to spend money on a silly picture, but I longed for it – so funny and cute, so not vanilla taffy.

I talked up the idea in the weeks leading up to our family trip to the shore, but my parents remained noncommittal. I even checked out a library book on caricature drawing so I could be discovered reading it and casually mention my interest in the artform. But my parents didn't really care what I was reading as long as I would put it away and go clean something when my lack of noise-making made them suspicious. So we went off to Wildwood, prepared for a whimsy-free vacation.

It was on our last day at the shore that my father paused by one of the artists on the boardwalk and asked me if I wanted a picture. I nearly threw my ice cream cone to the sand. I sat down, let my mother fuss at my hair, smiled widely and then stopped when my father shook his head – he didn't like how my smile squished my face. I tried to smize (I don't know what I called this pre-Tyra) and held steady. My neck grew stiff and sweat dripped down my back. My mother took my bored brothers away to look at carnival games they wouldn't be allowed to play.

At last, the artist handed me the finished drawing. I flipped the page over, hoping my tiny body would be riding a dolphin over the waves. I nearly burst into tears when I saw the sketch. The man who drew my picture was a portrait artist. His work was realistic and life-sized – no Colgate smiles, no friendly bold lines, no elfin bodies frolicking under physically improbable heads. He drew what people looked like, and he had drawn me . . . ugly.

The portrait was from an upward view and heavily shadowed the line that my brother and nastier classmates used as proof of my double chin. Every hair on my face was obsessively, finely detailed. My swarthy features and name had long ago awarded me taunts of "Priscilla Gorilla," and my mother's repeated attempts to wax and bleach my body hair hadn't improved my sensitivity around it. I was uglier in this portrait than I was in my reflection, and that was saying a lot.

My hands were folding, crumpling, as tears blurred my vision. My father's grip on my arm stopped me. He pulled the portrait from my hands and led me away, the pressure of his hand a searing ice.

My mother and brothers returned to hear him scolding me for damaging the portrait. I barely heard the words, focusing my energy on holding back my tears while simultaneously trying to will the drawing to spontaneously combust. One of my brothers took the picture and danced it around me, laughing. Even with my father's hand on my arm, I lunged for the portrait and grabbed it at the corner, tearing it part way down. My father nearly lifted me off the ground as he pulled me away, snatching the portrait from between me and my brother. Exasperated with both of us, he listed the punishments both of us could expect for making such a scene. None of it registered, except when he muttered, "That's what you look like, and if you don't like it, that's too bad."

He hung the portrait, which he insisted was well done, on the outside of my bedroom door when we got home. It stayed there for nearly a year. My father didn't waste money. Every time someone came over, they saw the portrait as we went to my room. They all made the same face, like they were thinking, "Why would you hang *that* up?"

I always think I'm over times like this, well-adjusted and mature. Until an ice-breaker activity at a workshop had my tablemate drawing a quick portrait that makes me look like a pizza pie wearing glasses and a mop toupee. At the moment of reveal, my breath lodged a fist in the back of my throat. I tried to laugh it off, waved away the artist's apologies (like, *OMG how vain do you think I am, please!*), but I looked down at my hands and noted only their lines, their ashy spots. I tried to focus on the presenter leading us through the next activities, the susurrus of whispered memories of my ugliness a constant background distraction. In the bathroom mirror, I could not stop my eyes from tracing the shadow of my moustache, my upper arm throbbing a faint, familiar ache like a misplaced pulse.

never forget

The thing about being first generation is that our parents always feel like visitors to some extent, but we're home. So when we are told that we can't do certain things – be too loud or too comfortable, too visible – we feel indignant. Entitled. When people tell us to go back to where we came from, we want to remind them that this "conversation" is happening on our front lawn. This is where we came from, this is the home we know.

I've kept touch with few people from my high school years, even fewer with any kind of closeness. It's tough, because I had friends and acquaintances that I liked, but I was so depressed and out of my body trying to keep the abuse in my home a secret, trying to put one foot in front of the other, that I don't even know who I was in high school. I watched all of it from a distance. I remember moments and interactions with sharp clarity, but it's like an actress playing me is standing in all the scenes. One thing I've found is that no one I went to high school with remembers the aftermath of 9/11 quite the way I do.

Kids would stop talking when I entered rooms or passed them in hallways. My immediate fear was that somehow they had found out about what was happening to me, and I was going to be known as a disgusting freak.

Hours later, after the quiet panic began to recede, I would start to connect some dots: people I had hardly spoken to in four years asking me where my family was from and what languages I spoke, acting as casually as three cartoon kids in a trench coat pretending to be one grown up.

I sat with a group of girls in the back of the room for what we sometimes called Slacker Science. On September 11th, just before the news came and our teacher stopped class to turn on the coverage, they were debating the likelihood that hot dogs were actually pigs' penises. They brought me in as deciding vote, sliding an illustrated ballot across the table.

The next day, as I went to take my seat beside them, three hands quickly covered up a note that had been passing between them. They were looking at me with desperate, *please believe we're acting normal* smiles. I stood up to sit somewhere else and one of the girls tried to stop me, insisting the note was nothing, just really dirty. They didn't want to offend me. I wanted to remind her about the pig penis debate. I didn't. I sat down and said little.

I only tried to talk to one friend about it at the time. I was at her house. The news was on. NBC was interviewing brown people in NYC about the increase in verbal and physical attacks against brown people in the US. Sikhs, hijabis, and Indians with American accents like mine, talked about being called terrorists, vandalism of their homes or their parents' homes or their places of worship, the fear of walking alone. "This is our home," many of them said, "it's the only home I've ever known."

Earlier that day, a young man from Egypt had been murdered as he worked the early morning shift at his father's gas station in Arizona. My own father reminded me not to remove the bumper sticker or vinyl miniature American flag flapping over the passenger side window. "People can't tell by looking at you," he had said, in what would be one of the four times he discussed racism with me.

When my friend came into the room, having found her shoes, she asked me what was wrong. I was crying a little, I realized. I told her that it was all making me angry, and afraid.

"What is?" she asked.

And I explained, about the attacks against people who are born here, who have no connection to our attackers, people like me.

"That's dumb," she acknowledged.

Emboldened, or unleashed, I went on to point out the hypocrisy I saw in the aftermath of Oklahoma City bombing.

That guy was white and it didn't mean that people went around beating up and screaming at white men, I said.

"Well, yeah, but the difference is that he was American."

I wanted to say: "So am I."

I wanted to ask her: "Shouldn't that make it even worse?"

But I didn't say anything. It was like the words had been slapped out of my mouth.

I talked to some online friends about the way I was feeling, and most did the online version of nodding sympathetically (*hugs*). One of these friends wrote that he didn't know why it was bothering me so much if nothing was happening to me.

And, I am so grateful that no violence came to our door. Our home was not defaced. No one directed racial slurs at me at school. None of my family members were physically attacked.

I didn't tell my friend about the man at Port Authority bus terminal who yelled out as I passed that he had something in his pants that would make me a patriot, and his friend who laughed and warned him that raghead pussy was so dry and sandy it would shred his dick.

I walked past them without acknowledging I'd heard them, but I chanced a peek through my hair when I reached the escalator. They were older than me, in probably their mid-thirties, with women who sat under their draped arms looking disgruntled. One of the women caught me looking and sneered, gave me the finger, and rolled her eyes.

I didn't tell my friend about the anxiety, either. Both of my parents worked in the city, one brother was at NYU, and the other was living in Midtown. The day of the attacks, they were all there. No phones worked. We could smell the smoke through the windows of our New Jersey high school, see its distant haze. I went home to the empty house, rushed downstairs to the garage that I knew would be empty.

They might be dead, I thought. *They could be. I wouldn't know.*

I realize now this same vague fear follows me when I don't hear from Kris during long, busy days. I wouldn't know, I think. You don't know until you know. You just have to wait. It's an irrational ghost of a thought, and like a ghost, it haunts.

I felt that same anxiety every day for months. In the middle of classes, with everything else I was trying to keep compartmentalized occupying the corners and basement of my brain, unruly thoughts would burst into mind.

Maybe they're all dead.

Maybe someone attacked Dad.

Maybe while Mom was walking into work, someone threw something from their car and it hit her.

These were things that were happening.

Not to me, I told myself.

And then: maybe just not yet.

I got my first collection of fairy tales at a yard sale, a yellowing tome with a peeling faux-leather cover. The gold lettering had mostly flaked off, leaving a shadow of the title. It cost 50 cents and the woman who sold it gripped me with knotty fingers and warned me that those stories were not like the movies.

I rode my bike as far from home as I dared to go then. A stretch of grass by a skinny brook at the bottom of the best hill, but to my suburban eyes, luxurious and wild enough that I privately called it The Meadow. I lay in the sunsplashed grass and opened the creaking cover of the book and I fell, hard. When I finally pulled myself away, I felt new. Armed. The woman had been right; the stories were not what I had heard or seen of fairy tales before.

There were witches hungry for child-flesh. The devil, sorcerers, handsome men who dismembered pretty young women. And there were parents who did the things that parents should not, families behaving as monsters. The children in those stories were clever, resilient, able to climb up from slicks of blood and thwart their tormentors before trudging off to a happily ever after.

Fairy tales were the first truths I ever read. My first glimpses at survival and a future. I knew as a kid that the world was born in fire and soaked in blood, and that monsters still roam, hungry and cunning. I knew that my bones would make their bread, that my hands would be cut off to repay their debts, that my death was locked in the hall closet, waiting.

Gretel lined my path with white stones, and Ashputtel taught me to work hard and keep my secrets. All-fur showed me the value of camouflage. Morgiana's quick-thinking and steady hands under pressure were my inspirations. I have been told throughout my life that stories are frivolous, but I know that they save lives.

The stack I can assemble from my bookshelves now is paltry. My true collection would tower above me. It's been scattered, books lost in moves or in the messy rooms of students. I still know where the original book is: on the shelf in my childhood bedroom, dusty, unread for years. I miss it – the decaying cover, the thick pages and the comically ornate font. Sometimes I wish I could go back for it, but I learned early that if you want to survive, you have to leave even the most precious things behind.

what doesn't kill you

The Monday after the mass murder at Pulse in Orlando, FL was the last day of classes before end-of-year testing began. Attendance was low and classes were loosely structured – test prep, last minute grade-savers, *can I please just read my book?* I had thought about the shooting all weekend, but I had no words yet.

I was teaching newcomers to the US, who had immigrated from countries in Africa, Asia, Latin America. Many of my students were Muslim. Many looked like the Latinx clubgoers who were attacked at Pulse. Many came from places where governments are corrupt, violence is public and frequent, where homosexuality is considered a capital offense, where gay people are proclaimed subhuman.

I only spoke to one of my students about the shooting. Luis brought it up to me, asking if I'd heard about it. I braced myself for a conversation about homophobia and respect; Luis was the kind of student whose anger and desire for attention manifested in making deliberately hateful comments for their shock value. I was raw and stinging underneath my skin, angry beyond coherent words, and I wasn't sure I could be calm enough to handle what he might throw at me.

I told him: I had heard about it. It had made me so angry, and scared.

Luis was quiet for a moment, looking at me thoughtfully. Then he said, "This stuff isn't supposed to happen here."

A friend of mine, another high school English teacher, confers with her students after their daily freewrites by asking them what they have written about and jotting quick notes in her log. On Monday, one of her 9th graders told her, "I wrote a list of reasons why people who don't know me might try to kill me."

"How am I supposed to write that down for my conference notes?" she asked me. "How do I even begin to say something that matters to that student?"

She also told me she had shared that story with a few friends, some teachers and some not. One of the fellow teachers said, "Oh, 9th graders are so dramatic."

I have made the same list. More than once.

Who I teach and what I teach and where I teach and who I am, brings me often to the intersection of politics of language, identity, religion, culture, feminism, and more. I'm often around adults who complain about "politically correct" thinking and language – that words will not change feelings and ideas, that these are band aids on broken bones, that oversensitivity is going to raise our children to be weak and useless. I have heard teachers use these or similar statements to justify their refusal to bring issues of race, gender, and sexuality into their classrooms.

Maybe the words I use and those I choose not to use will do

nothing about my own cynicism, my apathy, my held biases. But 12 years of teaching has shown me the power of words and how they influence mindset, openness, and thought. When I ask myself what I want my students to learn and take away from my classroom, it is never my cynicism, my lack of faith in humanity. If we want them to do and think and live better, then we have to teach them how.

Some people like that. Many do not. But it's not about us.

Teachers are discouraged from talking about what is happening around their students. Sometimes, it is test pressure. Often, it's that teachers aren't trained or prepared to have these conversations. Sometimes, there are direct orders from administrators, or protests from parents who do not want teachers pushing political agendas on their children.

Passing a test cannot be more important than becoming the kind of adult who has agency and knows how to maintain it, who both wants and can plan how to improve their world.

And maybe part of our problem is that people consider teaching students that everyone is human, everyone deserves recognition of their humanity, is a political agenda.

I don't have any answers, any profundities to share about the murders and massacres of our time. I am not an expert in bringing the real world into student discussions, in getting over or going through my own fear.

I have only the dread I carry deep in my belly, dread that my students navigate a world that sees them as less and less than what they are, that reduces them to slivers of their identities and shrugs about their rights to live.

I have that fear that I will walk into my classroom to find another of my students has been murdered or attacked because of their ethnicity, their clothes, their sexuality, their neighborhood. I have the certainty that we can and must do better.

That, and an aching raw wound for a heart. It still works, though.

such a nice girl

"But don't you miss your mom?"

I pause. The answer is resting between my tongue and my teeth, but it's not what they're hoping for. It's not the reply that will re-humanize me now that my image of normalcy, of niceness, has been fractured.

A few months after I stopped talking to my family, I started telling myself stories about where I came from. It was an old habit. I used to ride my bike, away and away, edging my tires along the invisible boundary of Too Far that I knew I couldn't cross. I pedaled hard and let myself glide, unspooling stories in my head as the scenery floated past: I was riding on horseback to escape my captors, piloting a biplane to undiscovered islands, leaning boldly over the railing of the crow's nest as my crew and I sought to explore the wide ocean. My bike stayed within the borders while I flew, built my new lives overhead: free.

Now, I was telling new stories, writing a new history. Walking alone or standing by the subway door, lulled by the rhythmic sway of the car, the shrieking of wheels against tracks, I dreamed.

I was an orphan, raised by nuns, kind but not maternal, caring but not terribly invested. I was fine, thanks.

I was far away, family across oceans, distant and neutral. Oh, no, really, I was fine.

I was the first of my kind. My mother was a tree; my grandmother, a mango. Yes, I was fine.

People tell me, "You know, being a parent is really hard. No one does it perfectly."

People say, "Everyone's family is crazy, though."

People say, "They must have done something right. Look how great you turned out."

I wish that one wouldn't mess me up so much. It is already confusing, sorting out what is *me* from what is *me, in reaction*, trying to wipe the fear and shame and lies off of what I had thought was a fond memory. Usually, after an attempt at such cleaning, I find there was nothing truly happy in the moment, after all. I am left feeling a little slimy, a little pruny, like I've just spent too long trying to wash a greasy pan under hot water.

I used to think I got from my father my love of old things, of huge structures, of open spaces, and from my mother came the meditative practice of cleaning something thoroughly and the unmatched satisfaction of savoring a spoonful of peanut butter over several minutes. I thought that I was funny because I mimicked my brothers' meanness, and that I was a good listener because no one wanted me to speak.

Everything I am, I had been told, was bestowed upon me by them.

Everything I am, I know now, I am despite all that could have drowned me out. Everything I am, I have earned and cherished, I kept alive even when my world was a bleak stone box.

People who have met my parents or seen photos tell me, "It's so clear how much they love you." Or, "I'm sure they loved you as best as they could."

Eyes go wide as I'm told, "I could never do something like that to my family. I couldn't handle how much it would hurt them."

I think about my cells, reshaping themselves around unfinished experiences, building organelles of anxiety. My body holds space for the routine and ritual even now, years later; my flesh replaced by the gears of an automaton waiting to perform its spectacular sequence. How it would hurt *them*, I think, and my laughter is tart and firm to the bite, green and bright like mangoes.

"I just can't imagine what I would do if my child cut me off like that."

Sometimes, when I've discovered a really easy way to clean the blender, or I pass a Kerala-style restaurant, I imagine what it would be like to call up the mom in the photos, the company version of her, and chat. I try to picture holiday gatherings at my parents' home, the Christmas commercial moments. It doesn't work. It goes wrong, like when you try to count your fingers in a dream and your hand turns into a fish. Maybe it's how things should be, but it's not how they are.

I don't see what other people see in the photographs. I resist explaining, pull away from the hunger for details. I won't play the justification game, seeking the validation of my experiences as "bad enough." I was there. I know.

Short answer: no, really, I'm fine.

dimples

We were watching Alie's daughter, Zee, careen around the Superbowl party, marveling that it seemed only days ago she had been crawling on those same sturdy, plump legs. As if on cue, she turned her cherubic face our way and broke out the killer smile that is going to get her out of *so* much trouble in the future.

"Oh my god, look at those *dimples*!" Laura squealed in delight, before looking up at my own smiling face. "Priscilla, you have them, too!"

I fought the urge to cover my face with my hands, a reflex from years of having my face pinched, squeezed, and poked. Laura, thankfully, made no sudden moves.

She had always wanted dimples, she told us. We laughed as she told us about sitting at her desk in elementary school, pressing her pencil's eraser into her cheek in hopes of leaving a permanent dent.

"I was like that with freckles," I said, recalling my attempts to dot my skin with pen, marker, makeup, paint.

Most of my life, I wished I could wake up in someone else's skin; no more chubby cheeks and dimples, no more explosive curls, every feature I'd bemoaned and hyper criticized melted away. I'd just be smooth and slender, unremarkable.

I was oft remarked upon. My parents regularly weighed in on my size and shape and appearance, ranging in their approaches from concerned tones to stern demands to exasperated yelling. Kids at school, even those I considered friends, made jokes about my fat, my body hair, and of course, those dimples. It didn't matter how many people told me I had a beautiful face and a warm, catching smile. One classmate trying to nickname me "Pillsbury Doughgirl" canceled it all out.

In sixth grade, this kid Roger would declare that he loved me in the middle of classes. He'd drop to one knee and profess his passionate desire for me. He would write notes that said I was beautiful and driving him crazy, and he'd get one of his friends to read the love letters out loud. The class would laugh so hard, and I laughed along to pretend it didn't bother me (because "stop" didn't work). That was the joke: that I was beautiful, that someone loved me. Get it?

Years later, he would tell me it was harmless fun. "I was just kidding," he said. "No big deal." Maybe it was harmless, all of it, but it matched what I believed about myself: I looked wrong, and it needed to be fixed if I wanted anyone to love me.

So I would set what I thought were goals – I was going to work really hard and become...someone else. That's the only way I can express it now, I just imagined turning into another person. I would look at models in advertisements or whoever was considered one of the "pretty girls" at school and just think, I need to be this. I need to be *her*, not *me*.

Even now when I smile at my reflection, I'm reminded of how for many years I stood in a very similar place and *hated* this face. I feel the aching memory of the pain in my jaw from sucking in my cheeks as hard as I could, trying to iron those dimples out (before I started avoiding my reflection as much as possible, eyes fixed on the edges of the glass while I brushed my teeth or dressed).

About a year ago, someone asked me to fill in the blank: *I feel beautiful when* _____. I just stared. The expectant line yawned, but I had nothing to offer it. I tried out answers I had found online, but not even Google could help me.

Then, I saw a video made by a high school student that had gone viral. The student had filmed the reactions of people who were told they were being photographed because they are beautiful. The responses are pretty much the same, with participants dissolving into blushing, giggly, grinning puddles of joy.

There is one exception, a young woman who is looking down when the photographer tells her they are taking photos of beauty. "Of what?" she asks, annoyance creasing the space between her eyebrows. The photographer repeats the statement and the young woman looks up, unsmiling. Her eyes settle on the camera as she says, calmly, "I'll cut you in the face." Then she smooths some balm across her lips, her eyes steady on ours.

That young woman is my hero. I made that moment into a gif. Every time I watch that moment, which has been many times and will be many more times, I think, *YES*. Because I want, more than I ever wanted to be beautiful, to tell other people what to do with their opinions about me.

I came to hate even the concept of being beautiful, to resent being defined at all by my level of beauty. Even when some of my features came into vogue and women wanted curls and curves, thicker brows, I balked at the invitation. "I don't want to be beautiful," I was saying out loud, while I added to myself, *Good, because you're not.*

I think about Zee often, how she is growing every day to make space for the fullness of herself. She is far beyond toddling now; she dances with her naked reflection, shows off her belly with pride and infectious joy, and reads picture books aloud to me while she lounges on her potty. Already she is tall and strong and brave; already, she is funny and clever; already, she is herself.

And I know that in the future, there will be those who want her to shrink herself. Half of me will want to laugh and wish them good luck, while the other half will want to let them know what I will do to their faces.

But in the end, it's not about what I or any of the adults around her will say to protect her or to make her feel beautiful. It's about what she will see when she looks at herself, how she will define beauty, and how we can help her write herself into that blank space.

callous

Miguel died in October. Walsh told me, 10 seconds before students would come in for first period.

"I have some bad news," he said, like he was going to tell me we had a meeting during lunch, or that he needed me to cover his class later. I was still smiling at him when he told me that Miguel had been murdered the night before.

The words bounced around my brain for a long moment, registering in different, remote parts of my body. Realization hit my legs first, the muscles tensing as my knees went soft with shock. The smile started to deflate and the hot trembling of my face seemed to startle Walsh, as if the news had finally sunk in for him, too.

Delayed, my hands floated up to fold protectively over my cheeks, my mouth, and I was surprised by the sound and sensation of my rapid breathing. I had thought the tightness in my chest was a plea for air.

Everything felt like a surprise then: I blinked and I wasn't crying; I leaned back against the table behind me and I did not collapse.

I stared up at Walsh, who towered over me. Miguel was nearly six-and-a-half feet tall, seemed to fill the doorway with his breadth, but I was thinking about the doodles he would incorporate into his freewrites in class: small stick figures, crooked and floating aimlessly among the lines on the page like his childlike handwriting, always smiling.

A noise came out of me, not the squeaky, broken thing I expected, but a gravelly rasp that I felt more than heard. Belly-deep. Bone-deep.

Later, after a long day of blurred rushes through time, classes passing in greedy gulps, Walsh came back to check on me. He draped his long body across one of the student desks. I leaned against the wall in the blind spot my students and I tried to shelter in during lockdown drills.

He told me about his previous job at a school in Brooklyn, "something like 20" students murdered over his years there. Gangs, robberies, accidents, he said to the ceiling, his hands laced to cradle his head, his voice flat.

"This was your first one," he said.

At the time, the floor tilted beneath my feet. I pressed my palms tightly against the wall as if I could secure myself there. Walsh's words made me light-headed, sick with judgement. I couldn't recognize, then, how he had learned to survive, how the repeated stress of pushing through builds a callous on the soft, woundable parts of you. I couldn't see that the surprise on his face wasn't at seeing something unusual in my reaction, but at finding it familiar and distant.

I have never been able to write about Miguel, not really. I have barely been able to talk about him. At work, people wanted to ask me how I was doing and speculate in the same breath. They wanted to tell me that they thought it was gang-related; "must have been."

I wanted to scream until I couldn't hear anything, until the sound was a live, angry thing that would pour out of me, rise up, and chase everyone away.

Leon, Miguel's brother, didn't come to school for months. For so long, there were these two empty spaces (the same seat in different classes, I realized when they were both gone). And then one day, after February break, Leon was back. Quiet, smiley, himself. He sat in a different seat, though. The old one stayed empty. He came to my room after school that week to talk about books. When he left, half-an-hour later, he said, "I missed it here."

I wanted to tell him he could talk to me, that I was there.

One day, in the middle of a comfortably chaotic class, he got up and moved back to his old seat. Their old seat. For just a second, my breath caught, my lungs squeezed in the fist of my stopped heart. It looked so familiar, so strange.

Months later, during a meeting, one of my coworkers told us there had been an arrest made regarding the murder. A student who had been on the roster last year but never showed up, discharged after a month. Lived in the neighborhood. Gang-related, "must have been."

I waited to feel something, staring at the shared chair, the student-drawn portrait of Miguel still hanging on the wall. They had drawn him broad and muscular, included his chains and tattoos and ever-present baseball hat. They had drawn him smiling.

taboo

I never learned how to fight.

Conflict in my house was explosive, stifled for fear of what the neighbors would think until it couldn't be contained. Then it was all screaming and slamming doors, china and trinkets shivering in their display cabinets. The next day, silence was smoothed back into place, over us, and the issue was considered dropped, forbidden to revisit. Whoever tried to continue talking about it was causing trouble for no reason.

Get over it. Let it go. Leave well enough alone.

Better not to say anything at all.

I was pretty bad at this, but I tried really hard to be good.

I tried to be quiet, to look happy, to not talk back or complain. I didn't understand when I was younger why I always felt so tired, why I would suddenly say things I knew that I shouldn't. Why I seemed to be watching myself through a two-way mirror, waving frantic, unseen warnings and cringing at what came out of my mouth.

I didn't know about stress and trauma, about why every day felt like a week to me. I just thought I was bad. "Not a piece of cake," as my mother would put it when she told me, years later, to forgive my abuser.

Conflict and disagreement was met with anger and violence in my house. I saw my options as avoid, or deal. Avoiding meant being quiet, swallowing words and feelings until I was nauseous and bloated. Dealing was done by gritting my teeth, crying and pleading but knowing the course wouldn't be altered.

Outside of my house, I avoided conflict by avoiding relationships as best I could. I didn't know how to connect deeply to people, and my behavior was manic and bubbly. I cultivated a weirdness, an annoying pep, and kept my interactions shallow. It wasn't a conscious effort, really. There was just so much I couldn't talk about: my family, my home life, what I had done after school or on the weekend, boys and sex and bodies. No comment, no comment, no comment.

It was easy, for so long, to be quiet. It made everything easier, in the short term. But I got older, and I became aware that I was living longer than I had ever expected to; out of high school, out of college. The friendships I had formed demanded more of me. I had met people that I wanted to share my surprise life with, loved ones that were building into a chosen family that would nurture and support me. And they needed me not to disappear for days at a time, to do more than shrug and smile my way through a conversation. They needed me not to curl into a snail shell when faced with a conflict.

I never learned how to fight with my fists, either. Growing up among boys, tomboyish into my teens, I should have been good at roughhousing. When we used to play WWF, the futon in his basement was the ring, and I had to play shirtless. If I complained about how I was touched, if I fought, he would kick me out of the game, isolate me to the hallway while the games continued. I would hear them playing through the walls. He would ignore me for days sometimes, get the others to go along with him, until I learned not to say anything, not to fight him.

It wasn't just wrestling. If I pushed him or hit him or bit him during any of his "games," he would make me apologize, tell me how mean I was for doing that when he was being so nice to me, taking such good care of me. He would tell me how much trouble I would be in until I apologized and let him continue.

Two years ago, at a self-defense workshop, I confessed that my fear in facing the suited-up avatar was that I would freeze. I didn't add the words hiding behind my wisdom teeth: "like I always have."

I didn't freeze. I bellowed and kicked and punched. Finally, I fought for myself. I walked out of that room feeling more proud of myself than I ever had, feeling like I filled every inch of my skin.

But I watch the video of my fight and see my restrained movements, feet and fists striking out with only a fraction of my force behind them. I can point to where my strength is gathered in the muscle but not firing, and I know I was holding myself back. Trying to be good.

I'm learning. I practice saying what I think to the wall just over someone's shoulder. I find that afterward, I'm almost always holding my breath.

Seven years in and I'm still testing the ground between me and Kris. When he says something I disagree with, there is always a pause on my end. In my head, I am saying, "Talk. *Talk*. Say words." My voice, a curled vine in the tunnel of my throat, cowers. The words are wrapped in the velvet skin of their buds. Sometimes, they bloom, their fruit falls from my mouth, their flesh is textured and flavorful. Sometimes, they wither and shrivel, their seeds rattling in the hollow spaces inside of me. I hear their echoes for days and lose myself in the sound.

hands

I don't have my mother's hands.

My mother's hands were the feet of small birds, slender and strong. As far back as I can remember, she lamented them. They were bony, she said, wiry with veins that she attributed to working them too much. She would take my own hands in hers, turn them over to reveal the palms and study them as if she were going to read my fortune.

"Your hands are so rough," she would say instead. "So many lines. You need to take care of them," she told me as she slathered Keri lotion on them, somehow keeping a firm grasp on my desperate, slippery attempts to escape.

I liked the lines of my palms, the feathering pattern that gave my hands texture. Grip, I liked to imagine, as I practiced my handstands in gymnastics class. I played witch in the backyard, mixing potions of dirt and leaves in empty flowerpots, pouring water through the tributaries of my weathered hands as I chanted nonsense sounds.

My mother's hands were always cold. They were smooth to the touch, though the word "soft" never came to mind. "Cold hands, warm heart," I told her once, but it was one of the many idioms she had never learned and she stared at me blankly for a moment before she explained, matter-of-factly, that it was most likely poor circulation.

Sometimes, her fingertips went pale and held the indentations of whatever pushed against them. I would press my own fingertip into hers and marvel at the convex shape it formed, like a shell for mine.

Now and then, someone will comment on my hands, complimenting me on the shape of my fingers. I always think first of my mother squeezing the pad of my thumb or the web below my index finger with an accusatory shake, of the hours I spent pinching at my own skin. I would open and close my fists over and over again, wondering if I could change them, make them smaller and more delicate, more like my mother's.

Like her, though, I pinch. I squeeze and crush — playfully, but it hurts, and when it does, I am dismissive. "Oh, come on," I say, or my face does, and it's so much like her. She liked to poke too deeply, grip too tightly, make you gasp or whimper and then roll her eyes at you. "It didn't hurt," she would say, and when I hear those words in my own voice, I wince, too.

We were different colors, we had been always, but our hands

seemed the most different to me. It's not true that they were; they were no more different than our faces, or our knees, or our feet. But looking at them side by side, or fingers interlaced, the pale buttery shade of her skin contrasted so sharply against my brownness that I wondered if I was even hers.

impact

"Who can remind everyone what 'impact' means?"

Hasan said, "Change," and Chi added, "Affect." Nico drove a fist into the belly of his palm with a *thwack*.

I felt myself get nervous when my Assistant Principal walked in to observe the lesson – the already warm room suddenly stifling, my shoulders magnetically drawn towards my ears. I tried to will myself calm, but the pacing was slipping between my fingers, a loose but determined unraveling.

The crash didn't come until the small group discussion, when both me and my AP paused to observe the same table. The extra attention probably contributed to their collective choke. After they fumbled for a few moments, we both tried throwing them a line.

"What is an impact?" my AP asked, prompting them to step back from the discussion question.

They stared blankly. I tried not to scream. Hasan – that

Hasan, the Hasan who had, just moments ago, confidently proclaimed "change" a satisfactory synonym – shrugged.

He *shrugged.*

My AP tried some personal examples, dropping hints, then asked again. They shook their heads. I sighed quietly and thought, *it's probably not too late for me to learn how to do latte art.*

Anya, who shares with me students, a classroom, and an endlessly supportive shoulder, pulled me outside at lunch for Chinese food and sympathy. Observations feel like trials: my worth as a teacher based on a handful of minutes in the middle of a unit of study, with approximately 30 adolescent wildcards to keep things interesting. And it was my first year at a new school. My *fourth* first year. I was trying to remember that the staff had hired me, that I hadn't been foisted upon them like an unwanted heirloom, like a gift they were waiting to return.

"I recognize that part of this is ego," I said, carefully, the steaming piece of sesame chicken I was juggling between my teeth threatening to scald me. "I don't want to be bad at this, because this job is, like. . ." I gestured wide with my free hand.

She nodded. "It's not a job. It's like an identity." She knows.

Later, on the train, Serena and I joked about our May brains, holey like Swiss cheese.

"Earlier, I forgot how to spell my name. I was like...is there a C in it??"

We laughed, and then I told her about my observation, "impact," Hasan's bewildered face. She rocked back in her seat, howling. My laughs came from deep, and I tipped my head back into them.

She wiped a tear from the corner of her eye. "Sometimes it's just. . ." She brought her fist into her palm with a *thwack*.

falling

I met Kris in a thunderstorm.

That's so much more romantic than saying we met through OkCupid. Although, credit where credit is due: back in our day, it wasn't an app yet. It was an actual, full-fledged website, with a message center and a FAQ and everything. You could basically say that we were penpals who fell in love as we wrote letters back and forth.

Or, you could say that we met in a thunderstorm.

I chose my former neighborhood pizza place as our rendezvous point. The morning air had been thick and grey, and I wanted to bail and hang out with my roommate, maybe sneak into the second half of a movie in the theatre where we had taken in a morning matinee. Not because I didn't want to meet Kris; I did. I was scared. I had a developed a routine with first dates, one that resulted in few second dates and my deliberate fading into the background. I insisted that it was what both parties wanted, that I wasn't significant enough to the man I had just gone out with for him to mind. Kris had been talking to me for two months, and I liked him, which meant it was about time for me to drift away. Meeting him felt like the beginning of the end, rather than the start of something. For a few long minutes, I stood outside the subway station, gazing at the heavy clouds that seemed to hang too low in the sky and wishing I could stay in this moment: with an inbox filled with messages from him that made me smile, with the potential sweet in the back of my mouth.

By the time I got to the Bronx, it was pouring. I sloshed down empty streets, curbside rivers flowing ahead, and arrived at the pizza place with unpleasantly warm puddles in the toes of my shoes and a commitment (which was immediately tested by a few overly friendly pizza shop patrons) to pretending my shirt was not completely see-through.

Kris appeared in the doorway as I was finishing my slice of pizza and freezing under the air conditioner. The man who had been staring at my chest since his lusty declaration of "God *bless* you," glowered sulkily at him as he squished over to my table and sat down. The rivers running down his face broke and rerouted as he smiled at me. "Hi," I said, and handed him a single, useless paper napkin from the black and silver dispenser, the wispy kind that lack defining characteristics of napkins, like absorption and the ability to clean.

He took it solemnly from my outstretched hand and thanked me, and I finally felt like I was getting warmer. I was smiling despite my efforts not to and the grin splitting my face was edged with an ache I didn't mind, like when the sun breaks through a dense cloud on a grey day.

I gestured to the still dripping sky outside and asked Kris if he still wanted to follow our plan for the day, a visit to the New York Botanical Gardens. He said some things that amounted to, "Yes, of course." We walked out together and I was already thinking that I wanted to see him again.

We found the Garden's 250 acres mostly deserted. As we rambled around, meeting no one else, I led us down a path toward the river running through the park.

"I hope neither of us is a murderer," I called cheerily over my shoulder. We stood beside each other at the riverbank, admiring the wild lushness a single thunderstorm unleashed, everything swollen and vibrantly colored. I nodded. "Yeah, because this would be perfect, " I said, and watched him from the corner of my eye. He held back a smile and I tried not to let my laughter escape through my nose.

We climbed a damp gravel path until we reached a clearing ringed by broad-leafed trees. It was late August but the leaves were already yellow, and the thunderstorm had laid down a thick carpet of gold. The whole space glowed in the pale grey afternoon. We stood at the edge of the hilltop, overlooking a pool churned by an adjacent waterfall, and he assured me that his ultimate plan was to throw me over the railing. He placed his hands on my waist and I gripped his wrists firmly.

"You jump, I jump, Jack," I said.

"What?" he replied.

The rain came and went, sprinkles and mist instead of the downpour that had drenched the morning, but it kept the crowds away. As we strolled down a broad empty path, he grabbed my hand. I teased him about wanting to hold my hand first. He pointed into the distance, indicating an employee golf cart puttering towards us, and deadpanned, "I'm just trying to keep you alive."

Later, when we had been roaming the park for hours, I reached up to his face and gently pulled away a delicate fragment of the paper napkin that had disintegrated when he used it to mop the rain from his forehead. He gazed at the feathery scrap in my pinched fingers for a moment, then looked me in the eyes and called me a jerk. It was the best date I had ever been on.

We would spend over 12 hours together, getting kicked out of the park past closing after surprising an employee, and finding our way to a nondescript bar in Midtown East on Karaoke Night. A group of French tourists sang earnest renditions of Nickelback songs while we took turns staving off hypothermia with the hand dryer in the single stall bathroom. Near two o'clock in the morning, a couple performed a version of "Barbie Girl" that was nothing less than performance art.

"This is so terrible," I said, beaming.

"Yeah," he agreed, grinning back at me.

Seven years later, even the trees were different. I walked beside him, comfortable in my sense of belonging, not thinking about what to do with my arms. We sat beside our waterfall, surrounded by groups of visitors who hovered impatiently while we squished together for a hundred selfies. I rested my chin on his shoulder and muttered, "Kick these people out of our park, please," but he only pulled me along to the gravel path up the hillside. It was a sunny summer day, and we arrived in the clearing to find it dimmer – no lush golden floor, the view blocked by a new screen of shrubbery. Side by side, we clung to the railing and leaned out, peering between branches trying to glimpse the water rushing below. Kris put his hand on my back, the touch at once soothing and thrilling. I let his warmth gather in the space between my shoulders, and when I leaned against him, I felt him press into me, too. We held each other up for a moment, and then I sighed.

"Hmm?" he asked, turning to me.

I gazed down at the overlapping layers of greenery below us, the water a restless grey shadow beyond. "It's going to be so hard to throw you over with all these trees in the way," I said, glumly.

He rubbed comforting circles on my back and said softly, "There, there."

wisdom

"OMG, Miss," Xio said gravely.

She was sitting beside me during lunch, following my Look, Don't Touch policy with my straightened hair. It's always a big deal the first time students see my hair straight, or that I wear contacts, or put on lipstick; any fashion deviations from norm are Hot Goss.

Xio's tone was alarming. I looked up from my grading.

"You have. A white. Hair."

Across the room, Katy gasped. So did I.

Then I said, "Wow! Where is it??"

They gaped at me as I pulled strands of hair into my line of vision, searching for the white thread.

"Um, you are not supposed to be excited about this!" Xio informed me.

"Why not?" I replied, still hunting. "Einstein had all white hair."

Xio threw her hands up in the air. "He was old! You're not old!"

"That's true," I noted, still hunting. "But Storm has white hair. And Rogue – in the new books she's younger than me." Xio had just gotten into *X-Men* and we loved comparing the most recent books to the ones I had grown up reading.

"They're mutant superheroes AND not real," Xio nearly shouted.

I was quick: "Except for REALLY awesome..."

We went back and forth like this for awhile, me patiently needling Xio while I searched for my elusive white hair, while she grew more exasperated by the word. Driving students crazy is one of my Top 5 Faves of teaching, so it wasn't exactly a fair fight.

Xio slumped across the desk. "Miss, you are so weird," she moaned.

"I am," I nodded solemnly. "But you knew that."

She sighed. "You're not supposed to like white hairs."

I dropped the cluster of strands I was examining and turned in my seat to face her. "Ok. Tell me why not."

She made a face. "Because it means you're old!"

I leaned toward her and stage-whispered, "But I'm not old."

She began to object but I kept on. "Also, being old isn't bad. It means I'm alive, and hopefully wise. That's pretty good stuff."

Xio scowled lightly. I knew I'd poked at her too much for her to give at all, so I smiled. "I can't find it, though, so I can't be that wise..."

The corner of her mouth lifted in the tiniest sprout of a smile, and she reached out to break policy and lift a strand of hair from my temple. It was half-white, as if it had been distracted midway. "Whoa," I said, holding the hair between two reverent fingertips. "That's pretty cool."

Xio smiled a little wider. "Yeah, it is," she said.

the heart

There's a vine at Bedford Park Blvd train station, winding its way around the towering steel columns that support the station house three stories above street level. Below, cars and buses thunder along the road, and the smell of gasoline and industrial-strength cleaner rises from the filling station and car wash on the corner. Up here, the vine coils tendrils around the wire mesh between the station walls, reaches out slender green arms to brush the heads of commuters climbing the stairs.

I've been watching that vine grow through the wall for 12 years. It has been a long time since that station signified home to me, but I work nearby every summer. Every year, it's bigger than I can imagine, and I am both delighted by its growth and a little sad to note how much time has passed since I've been back to my first real home.

My love for the Bronx, like my teaching career, began with my family's disapproval. My brothers attended NYU and lived downtown, so the Villages seemed the only sanctioned NYC locales in my family. When I graduated from college with no set plans, my parents welcomed me to move back in with them to figure it out.

Instead, I quickly found a teaching fellowship. My parents were not thrilled. My father seemed even more disappointed than when he found out I was majoring in "books and stories." Teaching wasn't the prestigious job they had looked forward to bragging about. They had moved 8,000 miles to be here; at least one of their kids had to be a doctor.

They made do, deciding to pitch the whole thing as temporary. My father informed everyone that his own father had been a teacher and a great inspiration to me (he died when I was eight and we'd met twice, but sure). They were starting to forgive me, a little, and then I got my placement in the Bronx.

They wanted me to withdraw. Not the Bronx, they told me. They shared stereotypes like ghost stories and snapped at me when I objected – they *knew* about these things, they had *been there*. My brothers chimed in, dismissing my opinions as liberal naiveté. Friends and neighbors were more gently skeptical, suggesting graduate school or gap years. My abuser insisted that the Bronx wasn't safe. The dim part of me that was fighting to survive had whispered, "Safe is where you aren't."

I found roommates and a house for rent, ignoring everyone's objections. My mother sniped that she'd never seen me not be lazy unless I was getting away from her. I thought that might be a pattern worth looking into, but I kept it to myself.

Nowhere feels quite as much like home as the Bronx. I love New Jersey, and I defend her dutily from those who would besmirch her name and label her an armpit, but going there feels more like visiting a favorite vacation spot than it does like going home.

When a workshop or weekend brings me back to the Bronx, on the other hand, I find myself eager to emerge from the train station to see that I've left Manhattan behind. I stroll, relishing the sprawl of streets, the grand architecture that rises palatial overhead.

The sky feels bigger, wider. One day, on a quiet side street, I stretch my arms into the empty space around me and a man across the way calls out, "Good morning!"

Question #1: So, where are you from?

When my mother moved to Washington Heights in 1980, newly immigrated from Kerala, everyone thought she was Spanish. I asked her what they meant by Spanish.

"Who knows? Port-o-rican, whatever." She waved a dismissive hand. "They talked to me in Spanish in the grocery store, and I told them, *No habla, no habla.*" No one knew where Kerala was, and when she said she was from India, she told me they looked at her like she was lying. I know that look.

Walking to the train station one night with my friend Bindiya, a man looks at us – our brown skin, my blooming curls, her slender arms – and calls out, "I love you, pretty Mexican women, I love you!" The shared laugh, the shared silence, feels as ancient and delicate as a prayer.

Question #2: Red dot or white feather?

My mother came back from India with a pack of decorative stick-on bindis, the kind I'd been asking for since I was six. My parents, mostly my father, saw wearing a bindi as a Hindu custom that he, as a good Catholic, would not endorse. But my mother had gone to India to bury her father, and part of her grieving process involved indulging her children – she had also smuggled home an entire jackfruit, the size of a sack of flour, in her luggage.

Delighted, I wore one of my bindis to school the next day, where a girl in my grade scoffed as we lined up to board the bus for a field trip. "Why are you trying to be like Gwen Stefani?" she snorted. Gwen had "gone Indian" in a recent music video, years before appropriating Harujuku style.

"Uh, I'm Indian, and these are *from India*," I shot back, in my best "you dumb" drawl. She flushed and muttered something while her friends took the opportunity to laugh at her. I boarded the bus with a mix of pride and shame to worry over, relishing the burn I'd delivered but conflicted about not having the right to it. There was one way that Indian women looked in pop culture then: lavish red and gold saris, miles of straight, shiny hair, ornate golden nose rings the size of most noses. I wasn't one of them. I wasn't one of anyone.

Question #3: What does being Indian mean to you?

In 4th grade, I was the biggest liar. It came so naturally, a marriage of my storytelling and what was already for me a constant need to lie.

I lied about my family. In my story, my real parents had died in a fire (I don't know what book I read this in, but I know myself well enough to know that it did come from a story and I was obsessed with it). I tried to make myself simply adopted, but I could tell my classmates were skeptical. They insisted that I looked too much like my mother, so I invented a convoluted plot worthy of the Malayali soap operas my parents watched after I was supposed to be asleep: my parents died, and our grieving relatives could not afford to care for me, so they put me in an orphanage run by kind nuns. Then, one day, a couple with two sons were shopping at the small store my uncle ran. He was amazed by how much the woman looked like his deceased sister and orphaned niece, and when he overheard the couple lamenting their lack of a daughter, he knew just which orphanage to send them to! "So, even though I look like my mom, I'm adopted," I explained.

"But you look *so much* like your mom!" my classmates repeated.

I sighed. "A lot of people in India look alike, I guess," I said, and they couldn't argue with that.

I lied about India. So much. I had a friend who was an elephant and the monkeys in my family's yard loved me so much they would come sit on my shoulder and sleep in my lap. I basically reimagined Disney's *Aladdin* to include me as the main character. It helped me connect with my mostly white classmates, and that, with elements of stories I loved, formed the vibrant, beautiful picture of my other life in India: a magical, different place.

I had really needed a magical, different place then. I had already given up on looking for reasons. I didn't know why the charming, cool older boy on our block, the boy everyone said was the most fun, had singled me out for his secret club. I didn't know why my brother was so angry about everything I did, from singing along to commercials on TV to wanting the same sneakers as him, or why my parents seemed so frustrated and disappointed with my . . . existence. Writing and counting and reading all helped, kept the things in my brain in their places so I didn't have to think about it all the time, so I could move and breathe, but nothing felt as good as telling the stories about my fake life. There was no one to contradict me – my authority was accepted by my classmates because the other Indian student in my grade had a different teacher – and so it could all be real. *This isn't really my life*, I could tell myself. *Somewhere, things are perfect and beautiful and just for me.*

Eventually, my parents found out about my lies when another mom called my house, unable to believe that I could be adopted. I looked, it would appear, *so much* like my mother.

"You are our child," she had assured me, in a low voice reserved for my least excusable behavior. I winced, still rattled from my father's yelling. "Do you want to see the scar you left me? Do you want to see your birth certificate?"

That night, I was distracted from my ritual of planning how to avoid another secret club meeting in his basement. I lay awake, miles from sleep. I told myself a story about my elephant friend. In the story, he was leaving, being sent away to another town. In the story, he reached his trunk through my window, wrapped it firmly around my waist, and carried me through the moonlight. In the story, we both got away.

Question #4: But where are you, like, *from*?

I remember being seven and my friend Amanda had come over to play. I was so excited she was there, because she was a cool kid before we really knew what that meant, and she had never come over before. We acted out wilderness survival games with my wide assortment of "creatively reassembled" (not *mutilated*) Barbies all afternoon. When I went down to the kitchen to ask if we could have snacks, I was surprised to find that my parents were angry with me. They hadn't expected that Amanda would stay for so long, and my father wanted to eat an early dinner and take a nap.

"Why doesn't he eat now?" I asked my mother. My father made a noise – surprised and unsurprised, at once – but said nothing.

"He doesn't want your friend to see him eating with his hand," my mother explained.

We moved when I was 12 to a smaller town. My parents enrolled me and my brother in CCD, evening classes at the local church, which commenced a few weeks before school started. It was walking distance to the rec center from our new house, but my father insisted on escorting us over and picking us up.

Scene: Summer evening, late August. The night is illuminated by the streetlamps and the bright headlights of waiting cars. Behind me, the windows of the rec center glow with yellow light that spills over the clusters of children who talk in small groups. My brother is nowhere. Everyone is with someone, except me.

Behind me, a group of 4 or 5 white tweens are talking idly. I have noticed them eyeing me curiously but I am pretending not to see it. At the center of the group is a short boy with a haircut that makes him look like a mushroom. He stands on the cement border of the rec center's lawn, placing him above the others.

Out of the corner of my ear, I hear snippets of the group's murmuring – they alternate between loudly sharing jokes, summer memories, and complaints about school starting, and attempting to whisper about me.

The boy with the mushroom hair finally calls out to me, and I put on what I think is the aloof, slightly annoyed expression of a glamorous actress in a Channel 11 afternoon movie. I can't remember exactly what he says, if he asks me about my ethnicity or if he already knows through the grapevine of this small town, but I remember how loudly he cries out, "Awesome! Does this mean we're getting a 7-11 here?"

By "this" he means me, I realize, my presence in this town he has probably lived in his whole life without talking to an Indian kid. Maybe any brown kid at all.

It is the first time that a stereotype like this has been applied to me, specifically. I know about it, obviously; I watch *The Simpsons*. But in my old town, there had been more Indians than just 2 or 3 families, and no one assumed we were all related or that our dads worked in convenience stores. I was often mislabeled as good at math, but that had really been the worst of it.

There will be much worse to come, but in this moment, I am stunned. No one has ever talked about my family the way Mushroom is.

I think his friends laugh. A girl calls him an idiot, tenderly, so everyone can tell how much she likes him. I can hear how she has practiced saying it, talking to her reflection when she is alone in her room so she can rehearse her facial expressions, the fall of her hair. I'm surprised by how much I can think when my brain feels so numb and my body has frozen me to this awful spot.

It feels like it is all happening at a distance, like I am underwater staring up at him as he continues speaking through the ripples: "No, I'm serious, I *love* 7-11."

Maybe I say something, something like, "My dad's an engineer," or, "No." My father finally arrives; my brother materializes beside him. I walk swiftly away from Mushroom and his group, realizing that under the knot of anxiety wrapped around my ribs, I feel the need to protect my father from these children. As we make our way back to our new house, he asks me, "Are those your new friends?"

[End Scene]

Question #5: How come you speak Spanish?

And even though I get it, I still snark sometimes, still roll my eyes sometimes. "I learned it," I used to say, coolly, hoping to shut down the conversation. I don't as much anymore. I tell the story now: school, novelas, Juanes, Cuba, teaching, Mexico, teaching, Colombia, teaching…

My student Kia said, "I don't understand what you mean that you don't speak your native language." Coworkers offered suggestions for clarification or rationale for her trouble, but I knew it wasn't wording or vocabulary. The concept of a cultural identity without a corresponding language was entirely foreign, as if I had declared, "I breathe milk," or "Left-hand Tuesday bathtub."

How does this happen? she was asking, regarding me with wonder and unease.

Working with immigrant students, the story is that family is enduring, and unbreakable: the Most Important Thing. Many of them come from families splintered or reunited by the crossing of borders, the pursuit of prosperity. As the child of immigrants without a family, I'm something of anomaly. A freak.

I was taught to remember that my parents had sacrificed for me, that their struggle to give me a better life had to be respected and honored.

At parties with my cousins, the children of other Keralan immigrants, we gathered in each other's American bedrooms to share our frustrations with our parents' insistence on maintaining their India rules, to do each other's makeup and hair, to listen to R&B tapes with the volume down low and dance in the narrow spaces between beds and dressers.

Downstairs, our parents sat in the living room, admiring the host's furniture and decor the way we fawned over each other's celebrity posters, complaining about their Americanized children and Anjali's moussed bangs. We didn't understand each other, parents and children, and I knew that *my* parents and I were not alone in this, but when I try to explain that it was so much worse, so far beyond, it's like I'm speaking a foreign language.

Question #6: What are you?

I struggle to express how it feels to be between cultures, to feel like I don't belong anywhere, because I don't want to offend or misrepresent any of the cultures I do have a foot in.

I worry that writing about my experience as an Indian kid in a predominantly white town maligns the people I went to school with and considered my friends, and erases the experiences of the other Asian people there.

And it's hard to talk about my family and separate our culture from my need for distance, because that relationship is not causal. But everything in a life, in a person, is intertwined and messy. I don't always know where the lines are, between traditions and harm.

And I wonder if, without family, I can even have this. What does it mean to be Indian without the parties in rented halls, without one hundred aunties and uncles who will all claim to have held me as a baby and ask if I remember them?

Without my mother walking me through our family recipes and scolding me every step of the way?

Without the eventual discovery that she made up half of the recipes because she forgot how her mother taught her, but it's ok because her mother did the same thing?

What is any culture, without the people who do all the same weird things you do, to gather around you and talk about how weird other people are?

Question #7: But where are you fro-o-ommmm????

"This is my grandmother's chicken," Hal said, lifting another glistening piece of raw meat from the tupperware container in my hands. I had been working with his daughter, Jaye, for a year or two, and the family had invited me to their summer home for a long weekend. Hal laid the chicken gently on the grill, swiftly clamping another in his tongs.

I could smell the flecks of rosemary, so I told him. "What else is in it?" I asked.

He shook a finger at me, smiling. "Took me a long time to figure this one out, young lady."

I laughed. "So, she didn't tell you?"

"Oh no," he said. "I had to try it out over and over, add a little of this, little of that. Took years."

He lowered the cover on the grill, placed the tongs into the empty container and took it gently from my hands. "After you," he gestured, smiling warmly.

For a moment, I thought of my own father, the way he would clap me on the shoulder after I'd helped him in the garage.

"I know what you mean," I called back to Hal over my shoulder. I paused to hold the side door open for him, turning to face him. "That's like my mother's chicken curry for me. I've never been able to make it; every time I try, something goes wrong."

Hal nodded, bowing his head reverently, knowingly. I found myself holding my breath, waiting for him to ask me about my family, my mother. Instead, he nodded again. "You'll figure it out," he told me confidently, and we went inside to check on the salad.

technicolor

"I think I'm going to dye the whole thing dark blue," I announce, tucking my legs up on the chair as the waiter takes our menus away. I twine a few bronzed curls around my fingers, offering them up as explanation.

"Uh, ok," Kris replies and I flop the hair over my face, laughing loudly.

"Thanks!"

He laughs, too, before adding, "I'm just surprised you're telling me. How many tattoos do you have now?"

He teases, with reason. I have a tendency to show up at the door freshly inked with a design I've never mentioned before, or to dye my hair while he sleeps in. He wakes up to find pink covering the blonde he'd just gotten used to, and compliments it knowing that it'll probably be purple in a few days.

He feigns concern for a moment. "Are you losing your independence?" and I cackle, burying my face in my hair again. It strikes me how much less time I spend in my head these days, how much more I say out loud.

I built so much of myself in secret, everything from hair dye to life goals kept safely locked inside, that using my words has been a foreign concept. The way they just fall out of me now, easy and light as air, it's like a whole new life.

happy

In 12 years of teaching, only one high school student has ever told me they wanted to teach English.

Some students have mentioned that they would like to be teachers. "But not English," they've always been quick to add. Serious eyes, emphatic headshake. Not English, the horror.

Most of my students can't seem to understand why anyone would be a teacher. "I don't have the patience," they've told me, usually following with the certainty that they would end up smacking somebody. I just smile, because they think that's where I spend all my patience. They don't know what I really need all this zen for.

A couple of years ago, one of my juniors, Wilfredo, asked me if he could talk to me after class. I always enjoyed talking with Wilfredo, who presented as generally too cool, strolling on the edge of wayward, but was clever and funny and kind of a sweet dork. So I smiled and said, "Of course," hoping he wouldn't ask about his grade. My stack of waiting-to-be-marked assignments, growing by the day, sighed wearily from my desk.

Instead, Wilfredo told me that he was thinking of becoming an English teacher. I couldn't measure my smile, but it was wide enough to have him bowing his head in embarrassment, giving us both a moment to get our cool back. He actually managed to do so; I was just giddy.

He told me that he had been thinking about his future lately, but also his past. He had come to the US knowing no English, but his accent was enough Bronx by the time I met him that I had assumed he had lived in New York since his childhood. "English isn't easy," he told me. He liked helping people learn, but he especially liked helping them with English. When he thought about his future, he told me, he felt like helping other people in a similar situation to his would be a good thing to do with his life.

"I think I'd be happy," he said.

I told you, kind of a sweet dork.

My face was still cracked open, so my initial reaction to all this was a firm YAY!!! But I gave myself a pause. Because this was not a declaration. Wilfredo wanted advice. He wanted to know, apart from the "economic issues," as he put it, if teaching is a good job. He wanted to know if it makes me happy. And I wanted to be honest.

I told him that teaching engages my whole brain, my heart and my breath, everything. I told him that I see the world as a teacher, that every article or movie or YouTube clip or meme I come across makes me think, if only for a second, about how I could bring this to my students. I told him that this job does not stay where you leave it, that even with the boundaries I have set around how late I will stay after school and what physically comes home with me, I can never just clock out or shut down. There is no off switch for the teaching part of my brain, I said, because it's pretty much all of my brain. Every year, I told him, I meet these fascinating people, and I get to know them, I share with them, and we become something of a family.

All of that, I assured him, is as demanding as it is rewarding. Sometimes – some months – some years – the giving outweighs the getting. This job makes me happy, I said, because learning is *amazing*.

It is amazing to learn and it is amazing to witness the learning of others, and as a teacher I get both. I don't know how many other jobs can give you that, because when I found this one, I knew that I was home.

So, yes, this job makes me happy. But it also makes me angry, and sad, and tired. I told him that this job is hard; that even though – depending on the state he lives in and the lifestyle he wants – he can do ok, he can live, those well-deserved holiday breaks and that hard-earned summer vacation will not lessen the demands this job will make. "That's just life, though, isn't it?" I asked him. "Nothing is just one way all the time."

For a moment, I imagined my life as a New York City dog-walker and I considered telling Wilfredo, "Run." Or at least advising him to do something in finance. I don't want to leave anyone with the impression that teaching grants you this pure, noble career, that the rewards of student achievement can counterbalance, let alone compensate for, the demands, demoralization, and abuse of education reform. It is easy to miss out on the joy of teaching, as things are; it is hard to grow.

But I wanted to be honest. And honestly, even with the

anxiety; even with the daily madness of working with 100 teenagers (and their 1,000 hormones each, and their completely normal adolescent ridiculousness multiplied by the trauma and anger and abandonment issues); even with the insult of being told by official after official, few of whom seem to know *anything* about teaching this subject or this demographic, that I cannot be trusted with my own professional growth; even with the knowledge that I could be a content dog-walker, this job makes me happy. That might not be enough, I know, but it's what I've got for now.

Wilfredo thanked me for staying to talk to him. I smiled again, and told him, "Anytime." The stack of unmarked papers cleared its throat, but I ignored it. As he left, I asked him how long he had been thinking about this, being an English teacher. He paused at the door, considering his answer over the muffled shrieks of exuberant 9th graders. "Since this year, I guess," he said. "You're a good teacher, Miss." He left and I laid my head down on the desk, pillowed on my arm, thinking that in this job, when it rains, it absolutely pours.

undercover

I can press 53 pounds of weight over my head with one arm.
I went from doing push-ups on an 18-inch elevation to floor
push-ups in 4 weeks. I swing, lift, squat, fly, curl, press, and
row iron in a variety of weights, four to six times a week. I
scramble up mountain faces, practice endurance through
yoga, kick up into handstands, and sometimes for fun, I hoist
my boyfriend over my shoulder, walking across the room
with his full weight on my back.

Basically, I'm strong.

The thing is, I have always had secret muscles. I don't *look*
strong. I don't have an "athletic build." Muscles don't jut
sharply from my resting limbs. I have a soft, protruding
belly; fat cushions my back and my ribs; my butt jiggles
when I walk; my arms look squishy; my thighs are BFFs.
When I flex, my bicep pushes up against a pocket of fat that
blossoms on my upper arm. I have given up puzzling at my
back in mirrors and videos, wondering if the ripples and dips
I see are firm gatherings of working muscle or layers of fat
bunching over them. My muscles are there and growing.
They're just doing it in hiding.

Some days, this is fine. I flex at my reflection and I can't help
grinning. I stretch and feel my growing muscles, and I'm
filled with the warm satisfaction of getting exactly what I
wanted.

Other days, this is so frustrating that I want to shatter all the mirrors in my house. I look at my reflection, pinching at my flesh, and I think to myself, *you are a disappointment.*

It's taken me many years to realize that those are not my words, and they don't come in my voice. They are the lies I was fed and raised on, so that I learned to ask for them by name.

Be smaller, everyone told me, through the clothes purchased in aspirational sizes, the diet plans, the costume changes during celebrations turned into photoshoots. Be smaller, the demand underneath the insistent, "We tell you these things because we love you." I tried to stretch my mouth around those words but it always came out wrong. I didn't want to be small.

I wanted to be Mowgli from *The Jungle Book*. Or some kind of wolf-girl. I wanted to grow up to be naked and dirty, to live with ferocious beasts. I wanted to be Max from *Where the Wild Things Are*, only I wouldn't make his mistake: no getting back in my little boat and sailing home for dinner; all wild rumpus.

I longed to scale trees with ease, keep pace with running deer, melt into the shadows and never be found. I wanted civilized humans to glimpse me at a distance and be too terrified and awed to try to follow. I wanted to be strong.

When I was eight, I lived for gymnastics class. The uneven bars, the momentary feeling of flying as I launched from one to the other. I never feared that I would miss, even though I did now and then. I relished catching hold of the bar, catching *myself*, pulling my body back and up and over.

I loved the beam, too, especially cartwheeling on the narrow space, grasping for balance with what my classmates called my monkey feet. I plummeted fearlessly from that beam, over and again, once crushing my wrist and fracturing it in three places. As I waited for my mother to pick me up that day, I used the injury as an excuse to practice one-armed cartwheels, to my coaches' great annoyance (apparently, you're supposed to sit still when you break a bone, and just falling on your face instead of catching yourself with your broken wrist is not considered a sufficient compromise).

I quit later that year, when it was pointed out that I was fatter than the other girls in my group and I didn't look as good in my leotard as they did. But I loved it while I did it. I loved tumbling and pressing up into handstands. I loved the feeling of my legs pumping as I ran at the horse, the gathering of my muscles echoed in the compression of the springboard before the launch. Then: up and over, splits in midair, maybe an attempt at a tuck. I loved being strong.

When I was in high school, I ignored the fat-loss diets I was expected to follow and crept down to the basement when I had a chance of being alone to lift weights. My brothers were both into body-building then, but they didn't like me to touch their equipment. I taught myself simple movements from what I saw on TV and in their fitness magazines. I would stand in front of the mirror, flexing a bicep or examining my quads, and I would feel a fierce pride. It was a secret, my strength, and I loved it.

And I loved a mosh pit, where no one was afraid to throw their full self at you, no one was worried about whether or not you could handle it. From local shows in church basements, VFWs and American Legion halls, to bigger concerts at Roseland Ballroom or out in Old Bridge, I collected sore muscles and bruises as avidly as I did pins and patches to decorate my bags. Meg drove us most weekends, in her mom's minivan or the hand-me-down, radio-less car I called "the Delorean," where I held a boombox in my lap so we could blast mixtapes. She tried crowdsurfing a few times, but that was never for me. I didn't think twice about how people saw me once I was in the pit; I just savored my strength and went all in.

The moments in which I felt strong stood out to me, bright like stars, thrilling like fireworks. They glowed despite the shadows in which I was ensnared. The abuse predates my memories. His grooming of me began when I was very young, and so did my self-destructive behavior. When I was older, I would wonder why he had chosen me. Of all the children in our neighborhood, all of the others who gathered in that basement for Nintendo tournaments and fort-building, I don't know what made me stand out. For a long time, I believed he must have seen something in me, recognized a fault that I couldn't see myself. I believed, somehow, that he knew me and what I deserved.

Despite the role of the helpless, damaged soul he played when I finally confronted him and told my parents, he is a masterful manipulator. He was always welcome in my parents' home and in the homes of all our neighbors – the families had been friends for our whole lives. I played right into the part he wrote for me. From the outside, we appeared to be close. It was *nice*, that we had been good friends for so long. It was *nice*, how he supported me and looked out for me. He had created this version of me, a *nice* girl. I knew all her lines.

I felt complicit, responsible for the abuse, and the longer I didn't tell anyone, the harder it became. I tried several times to convince him to stop – the earliest I remember, I was six years old – but eventually, I gave up any hopes of a normal life. I was too far gone. No one was going to believe me, or let me ruin years of friendship between families. I resigned myself to an eternity of being someone else's object – the shame and self-loathing were so deep that it felt like that was all I had.

Even as I forged ahead in college, the road was dark. I had no image of my future self. People around me had five and ten year plans, while I couldn't see to the end of the day I was living. I tried to stay away from him as much as I could, but I knew it was an inevitability: being cornered and isolated, being raped, feeling guilty, being made to comfort my abuser as he apologized, feeling guiltier. I crawled forward, got a job right out of college, moved away, got into therapy. I didn't feel strong. I felt exhausted. It's only when I look back now that I can see it: I had to survive, and I did.

I would be lying if I said I don't fantasize about what I would look like if my abuser had never targeted me, if I hadn't grown up feeling disgusting and wrong and betrayed by my own body. I want muscles that I can see on a body built by my own hands.

But I want more to climb mountains because the wild thing inside me still craves the rough scrape of stone beneath her palms, the tranquil moments at the summit, looking down on the backs of hawks.

I want the warm satisfaction that comes when I stretch and feel my growing muscles, and I realize I'm getting exactly what I wanted.

I want the joy of lifting heavy things because it confirms the truth: I am a force and no one has power over me.

"You're so beautifuuuuuuuuul!" sang Fleur, one of my 9th graders, as she danced around the classroom after school. The shrill melody wafting up from the ice cream truck four stories down was drowned out by her joyous warble.

We grinned, busted moves with her between cleaning and organizing and checking on the progress of the few other students finishing essays on that summer-scented Friday.

Planning as best I can, with an expectation of getting sidetracked, rerouted or lost, has helped me do meaningful, impactful work for many years. But even with the effort to prepare for surprises, there are times I'm shaken off that path. I fall into a pattern of anxiety that places me at the center of everything, trying to hold all the pieces in place.

There, cut off from the power I can wield when I am in my own place, the world distorts around me, swells into unfamiliar shapes. I find myself lost in what should be routine, stumbling where I usually glide.

That Friday, Fleur's science teacher remarked on her good mood, a turnaround from earlier in the day when her misplaced homework had her near tears. She apologized.

"But I can't do anything about it! I left my brain at home today. All I can do is put on some music and dance!"

I had been holding on hard to the behavior of a handful of students during that day's lesson, aware that my own anxiety about our current project was affecting my perspective. But what could I do about it, 4 pm on a Friday afternoon with sunshine and ice cream truck music streaming through the windows? Fleur turned up the volume and we danced.

acknowledgements

There is a meme you have probably double-tapped on Instagram, about how a person cannot realize their full potential without being fully supported. I am fortunate to have gathered around me a family that bolsters me, reassures me, carries me over waves of self-doubt and insecurity. To all of you: I am so grateful, I love you deeply, and no words will ever say it right or enough.

Thank you, Erin Brown, who never let me think this was anything other than possible. Your unwavering belief in this project allowed me to tentatively trust in it, myself.

Thank you to my early readers, Alie Stumpf, Pooja Bhaskar, and Anna Lurie. Your thoughtful, incisive feedback made this book, and me, better.

Thank you, Christy Kingham, for your tireless and insightful editing. You made each word shine.

Zulema and Jason, thank you for celebrating this project in style! Our reading was a beautiful show of support that carried me through the final steps of this process.

Rivka, Bindiya, Mari, Jen, Kate, Tom, Jocie, Ryan, Jenna, Chuck, Ben, thank you for being everything I needed in a family, for holding me when I did not have the strength to hold myself. My voice flourishes with you, and I love you.

Thank you to Patti Feuereisen, for your eyes and thoughts, for your strong heart, strong voice, and strong arms.

My Writing Project family, which grows year by year, thank you for providing me so many opportunities to try sharing my words and taking up space. You have all helped lead me back to my words, time and time again.

Kristopher Kennington, you have never faltered in your confidence that I could, and must, do this. Your steady, sure love has been my beacon. Thank you for showing me the way home.

ABOUT

Priscilla Thomas is a writer and teacher currently residing in New York City. *Gathering* is her first book.

71580922R00085

Made in the USA
Middletown, DE
26 April 2018